T0113424

Stress and Your Child

OTHER BOOKS BY BETTIE B. YOUNGS

How to Develop Self-Esteem in Your Child: 6 Vital Ingredients

Keeping Our Children Safe: A Parent's Guide to Emotional, Physical, Intellectual, and Spiritual Wellness

Safeguarding Your Teenager from the Dragons of Life: A Guide to the Adolescent Years

A Stress Management Guide for Young People

Problem Solving Skills for Children

Getting Back Together: Creating a New Relationship with Your Partner and Making It Last

Self-Esteem for Educators: It's Job Criteria #1

You and Self-Esteem: A Book for Young People

A Stress Management Guide for Educators

Stress and Leadership: Managing Your Response to Stress

Is Your Net-Working? A Complete Guide to Building Contacts and Career Visibility

STRESS
AND
YOUR CHILD

*Helping Kids Cope
with the Strains and
Pressures of Life*

BETTIE B. YOUNGS, Ph.D., Ed.D.

Fawcett Columbine / New York

A Fawcett Columbine Book
Published by Ballantine Books

Copyright © 1985, 1995 by Bettie B. Youngs

All rights reserved under International and Pan-American Copyright Conventions. Published in the United States by Ballantine Books, a division of Random House, Inc., New York, and simultaneously in Canada by Random House of Canada Limited, Toronto. Originally published in different form by Arbor House Publishing Company in 1985 under the title *Stress in Children*.

Grateful acknowledgment is made to John A. Ware Literary Agency for permission to reprint "The Two Stress Cycles: Distress and Wellness" from *Stress Management: A Comprehensive Guide to Wellness* by Edward A. Charlesworth, Ph.D., and Ronald G. Nathan, Ph.D., published by Atheneum Publishers in 1984. Copyright © 1982, 1984 by Edward A. Charlesworth and Ronald G. Nathan.

Library of Congress Catalog Card Number: 94-90598

ISBN: 978-0-449-90902-7

Cover design by Richard Hasselberger
Cover illustration by Patrick McDonnell
Text design by Mary A. Wirth

Manufactured in the United States of America

146903027

It was the first day of kindergarten for five-year-old Norma. Too shy to ask the teacher to use the bathroom and too timid to leave the classroom without first getting permission, she now sat at her tiny desk, crying because she had wet herself. It wasn't long before other students heard her soft whimpers and began staring in her direction. Some students, finding her predicament funny, snickered; others were relieved that it had happened to her and not to them. Some laughed purposely to be cruel. But one brave little classmate did not. Instead, little Norman got up from his desk, confidently walked over to the teary-eyed little girl, and took her hand in his. "I'll help you," he said tenderly. "And I won't let anyone laugh at you anymore." Turning to his classmates he said, with empathy uncommon in children his age, "How would *you* feel if it happened to you?" No longer feeling overwhelmed and alone, Norma now knew her dilemma was not the end of the world. She had an ally, a friend, a supporter, a helpmate.

That little boy and girl have grown up now, but Norma never forgot Norman, nor he her. Their friendship is now celebrating its thirty-sixth year.

This book is dedicated to Norma and Norman,
and to others whose kind actions serve
to buffer the stress of others.

Contents

Acknowledgments

W hen Bill Thompson of Arbor House invited me to visit
with him in his New York office regarding the effects of
stress on children, the conversation quickly turned to his concerns about the stress and strains his then six-year-old daughter
was feeling as she left the safe and comfortable nest of home
and headed off to school and all-too-competitive enrichment
activities. He feared these environments were serving up
stressors overwhelming for his daughter, and he wondered if he
could or should shield her from some of them. We talked about
the *new* stress, strains, and pressures that had permeated children's lives, and how more and more children were being derailed by the debilitating effects of stress. As a result of our
conversation, I wrote *Stress in Children* and Bill published it.

That was in 1985. Much has changed since then. Today's fast-paced society is characterized by clashing dissonance and exhilarating change at *every* level—at home, in the workplace, and in the world—each with ramifications for children. Shifting mores, changing family patterns, increased work and life-style options, the electronic age—all have shortened the once-guarded period of childhood innocence and served up a new "reality" for children—one that exacts from them a high toll. So when Ballantine publisher Joëlle Delbourgo asked that I reexamine the forces of contemporary life and the ways it exerts pressure and creates stress for families and children, I readily agreed. A very special thank-you goes to Joëlle for her vision and leadership in the inception of this completely new book, and to editor Lesley Malin Helm for safeguarding the integrity and mission of this work. It was a real pleasure to work with the Ballantine team. A heartfelt thanks to my agent, Julie Castiglia, for her tough professionalism and absolute encouragement over the years. Thanks for all you do, Julie.

As always, I acknowledge the love and support of my parents, Arlene and Everett Burres. Though we live a couple of thousand miles apart, each of my parents is a powerful anchor in my life, as is my magnificent daughter, Jennifer, and her father, Dic Youngs. I reverently acknowledge my brothers Mark, Kevin, and Tim, and sisters Judy and Laurie—they are genuinely honorable people and perhaps the best parents I have ever observed. Each has been a reliable source of unconditional emotional support, enduring love, and loyalty. These deeply rooted anchors keep me *safe* in many ways; a loving and supportive family is a real buffer to stress.

Many friends were highly visible and meaningful in my life in one way or another during the course of writing this book. In particular, I would like to thank two lifelong friends and associates, Mary Louise Martin and Mary Willia. I love these two women dearly; they know where the bones are buried and, lucky for me, fervently guard the gates. A very special thanks to a long time friend and confidant, Phil Salley, for his endless listening and feedback on the conceptual framework of this book; they were greatly valued, as always. And to friends John Wingo, Mark Victor Hansen, Jack Canfield, Lynn Fox, Betty Hatch, Sue Goodell, Christine Ferran, Tony Robbins, Vic and Bev Risling, Michael Popkin, Dave and Mary McGhee, Helice Bridges, Patrick Cavanaugh, Ken Pelletier, Suzee Vlk, and Michael Leon, for frequently checking in to see how I and the manuscript were faring. I greatly valued their insights and caring. For the wisdom and counsel of attorney Jenny Hawkins and Steve Lorber, a very special thanks; they are dear friends and look out for me.

To playful friends who nudged me into preserving playtime, a spirited thanks goes to Tommy Groff, Yvonne Oberly, Bill DeLeeuw, Debra Jones-Leon, Tom Dixson, Sandy Shapery, Roger Norman, Sr., Sassan Chakamian, Tom Sharrit, Paul Tammen, Debbie Walls, Rick Torres, Tommy Dobran, Sam and Jamie Ramey, Brian Gillis, Paul Thoryk, dear friend Larry Mabee, Jim Doan, Laura, Roger Jr., and Elise Norman, John Stinson, A. A. MacNaughton, Nancy Brandt, Lee Johnson, Karen Zovanyi, and John Moore. And for matters of the heart, thanks to Christopher Castillo, who performed magic—in more ways than one—and my number one-and-a-half, the "There you really do have it!" man, Greg Becker. Alas, some men really *are* more perfect than others!

To Linda Anne Kahn, Bilha Caidar, Karina Pawlukiewicz, and Pam Fawez, whose healing hands and loving hearts kept my inner and outer energies aligned. To Marie Rios, a loving and giving woman who makes my life easier; the spiritual goodness of her presence is always a gift.

Stress and Your Child

Introduction

I first began to examine the thesis that children experience stress and to document the effects of stress in the childhood years when I was a classroom educator during the seventies. The school has always been a convenient setting to measure how children are faring: In place are norms for scholastic achievement, expectations and standards for appropriate behavior, and guidelines for measuring how children interact with others. A host of professionals—the classroom educator, school nurse, counselor, principal, vice-principal, support and special service personnel—all observe children on a somewhat regular basis. Because the school is a place where one observes, sorts, ranks, and rates children, it's fairly easy to detect when a child fluctuates and deviates from those norms deemed *typical*.

Academic performance and emotional demeanor are not all that gets chronicled. Schools are often a source for vital health statistics on children, and school officials keep accurate records of students' school attendance, a source rich in information (and implications) as to how children are faring in their families and neighborhoods.

In the late seventies, schools began to struggle under the challenge of finding ways to encourage children to attend school on a regular basis, to behave in school, and achieve there. The biggest task was to convince students that graduating was in their best interest. In the eighties (during my tenure as a university professor in educational administration), the challenge was much the same—how to reduce the number of kids who would rather spend the day at the beach or hang out in their neighborhoods instead of coming to school. There was a noticeable difference, however: an alarming increase in discipline problems, and in the number of students visiting the nurse's office for illness and the counselor's office for psychological caretaking. In response, a number of major national studies came out, complete with recommendations for improving the nation's schools. Unfortunately, the much-touted reforms did little to curtail the number of youths who were permanently heading out the school doors, nor did it significantly increase the number of students experiencing scholastic success. On the contrary, the appalling number of students absent on any given day continued to increase, test scores continued to decline, and more and more children needed psychological counseling.

Many of the reform measures missed the mark because they concentrated on scholastic achievement and failed to address the underlying social problems that plagued children's lives. For example, more and more children were experiencing chaotic or broken family lives; were derailed by drug or alcohol use; or were rebelling, confused by the inconsistency between the words and the actions of parents, educators, and the media. Children's lives were now overwhelmed with stressors, each snowballing into problems far too complex for schools to address.

While mass and widespread attempts to improve scholastic achievement of the nation's children proved generally hopeless, these efforts did manage to highlight the poor conditions of the schools. Not only was the mission to educate children left wanting, but kids weren't faring so well either. Students were hurting—intellectually, physically, emotionally, and spiritually. When the spotlight was turned on the schools, it revealed that there were many despondent or often angry young people. Instead of children who were happy and had a zest and zeal for living, learning, and playing, there were signs of emotional duress too obvious to miss: increasing health problems, lethargy, sadness, melancholy, low self-esteem, an absence of goals, a sense of uselessness, hopelessness, despair, anger, and a real lack of inner joy and outer expressions of it.

Why was it that when we were doing more, things seemed to be getting worse? Aren't children supposed to be joyous, energetic, and mischievous? Where had all that gone? Why were so many children showing signs of anger or apathy or both? Why were so few of these young people laughing and learning and being joyful? Why were youths inflicting violence on fellow students? Why were they living what seemed to be lives of quiet desperation? *Why* are children's lives so stressful?

The results of my examination of the nature of stress in children was a book published in 1985 by Arbor House called *Stress in Children*. From its acceptance in the United States and abroad, I knew that others, too, had dispelled the idea that children were immune to stress and its consequences. I conducted hundreds of workshops in the States and abroad and the message was the same: More and more children are showing signs of increasing stress, strains, and pressures too obvious to dismiss. The notion that stress is present only in the high-powered world of the emotionally burdened business executive working under pressure was adjusted: Stress can affect anyone, regardless of occupation, status, or age.

Today, the toll of stress on children may be even greater than we suspect. One of the most significant and disturbing trends of recent years is the troubled generation of children who, according to a *U.S. News & World Report* study, are "unable to cope with the pressures of growing up in what they perceive as a world that is hostile and indifferent to them." The statistics bear sad witness to this fact:

- More than one in three children suffer stress-related illness, including dizziness, chest pains, wheezing, stomach problems, and headaches.
- There are nearly 2,000 teenage suicides a year.
- Fifteen percent of high school students are considered problem drinkers.
- One-third of all American schoolchildren under the age of 18 use illegal drugs.
- One-third of all violent crimes in America are committed by people under 20 years old.

- Students carry an estimated 270,000 guns to school daily (homicides committed by 15-to-19-year-olds increased 61 percent between 1979 and 1989).
- The school dropout rate continues to soar each year (it is now nearly 40 percent).
- Each year one out of every ten teenage girls between 13 and 17 becomes pregnant (more than one million).

It is distressing to learn that our children are experiencing this much stress, that they have so many debilitating fears and anxieties, that they worry more than we might suspect, that they wish to be happier. It's disconcerting to discover that in their desire to escape from pain, many children today (and at a younger age than ever before) take routes such as alcohol and drug abuse, delinquency, sexual involvement, acts of aggression and violence, running away from home—all paths that lead them into problems more overwhelming than those they are trying to escape. Yet it's not as if parents are unaware of their kids' difficulties: One in eight parents believes his or her children have mental or emotional problems; one in twenty parents admits his or her child has a drug problem.

There are no easy solutions to reducing stress in children, though it helps to understand children as social beings and to recognize the ways in which children develop and mature in each stage of growth and development. It also helps to understand the cultural revolution that is transforming so much of American life—spawning new mores, shifting values in the homeplace and the workplace, and redefining roles for both children and adults. Precisely because today's times do give rise to many inconsistencies and contradictions for children and offer up a constant barrage of new and changing experiences for them, children *need* our help and guidance—more than ever. We must give our kids a diverse array of skills, some of which we may still be seeking to master ourselves. The good news is that with our help and guidance, children can acquire the necessary insights and skills to surmount life's challenges. Those children who do learn self-awareness and effective methods for managing their response to stress, pressure, and strains are more likely to be healthy and happy, possess a zest and zeal for living, develop a healthy self-esteem, and lead fulfilling and rewarding lives.

The Stress, Strains, and Pressures of Contemporary Society

Chapter 1

CONTEMPORARY SOCIETY
IS NOT FOR WIMPS

O r the handicapped, or the elderly, or minorities, or. . . . Almost anyone would have a particular brand of hardship, or difficult experience, or oppression ready to complete the sentence. Virtually no one feels free from stress these days, not even young people supposedly living "the best years of their lives." Childhood innocence is now almost impossible to sustain. Many facets of life once regarded as for adults only—its mysteries, contradictions, tragedies, sexual and social responsibilities—are no longer off-limits to children. The accessibility of the electronic media, disruption of the nuclear family and loss of the extended family, increased mobility and home-shifting, elimination of old forms of labor and new work and life-style alternatives, changing mores, and shifting values in family life—

all these are quickly altering the nature of childhood. Nothing has been left unchanged; enormous social, economic, political, and spiritual forces have contributed to vast and sweeping changes in the home, at work, and in the world.

From the macro to the micro, there is a rethinking of how things should be, from quality of life to the human experience. These new expectations produce anxieties and render up a new brand of stress quite different from the kind we knew and for which our parents had to provide support and counsel.

Contemporary society is likely to catapult children into unprecedented stress. According to the National School Safety Center, the statistics bear this out:

- Every 8 seconds, a child drops out of school.
- Every 26 seconds, a child runs away from home.
- Every 47 seconds, a child is abused or neglected.
- Every 67 seconds, a teenager has a baby.
- Every 7 minutes, a child is arrested for a drug offense.
- Every 36 minutes, a child is injured or killed by a gun.

"When I Was Your Age, I . . ."

"When I was your age, I had to hike ten miles through a howling snowstorm to get to . . ." Did you smile as you read that line, perhaps remembering when you yourself dramatically acted out the part of the Pioneer Schoolchild, trying to compare your children's hardships with those of your own childhood? You did your best

Sarah Bernhardt routine, no doubt, attempting to make your children (who might have been complaining about their overload of homework, or cleaning up their room) realize how much better and easier their lives are than yours was. That's every parent's fondest wish, that our children have better, easier lives than ours. We try to provide our children more advantages—everything from a better education to the latest Nintendo release. Most likely, your children have more clothing, more games, more educational opportunities—even more vacations—than your parents were able to give you. But are their lives necessarily better, easier? Look at your children objectively. Are they as happy as you were when you were a child? Perhaps more to the point, are they as carefree as you were? When you played with your dolls or your trains, you did so more secure in the fact that you had a definite role in your family, that your life would follow a more or less prescribed course, with you in charge of the game plan.

We no longer live in a stable, predictable society. When you were in school, you believed there would be a fairly precise and constant course for your life. Your formal education was intended to carry you through your entire life. Not so today. The high school student is told that his or her diploma is nearly worthless in the marketplace, that employers have virtually no openings for someone with only a high school education. A recent high school graduate finds himself competing against not only college graduates who can't find jobs but against elderly people who are looking to supplement their retirement pay. Imagine how it must feel to have spent twelve long years in school only to be told you must continue your education or settle for a menial job with no security.

Even college graduates cannot settle back and expect life to take a predictable course. Recent graduates are told that they will have to change professions—professions, not just jobs—six to eight times in their lives. They hear and believe that they will not surpass their parents' standard of living or earning potential. Many will not be able to afford homes with the big backyard and swing set that they themselves had as children.

And let's not forget the cost of education. With some colleges costing more than $100,000 for a four-year program, there is little chance that most kids can pay their own way by busing tables. They go seriously into debt and worry about ever being able to repay their student loans. Perhaps they watch their parents go into debt, and worry that they will not be able to make it up to them. Take the case of Michael, born to older parents in a second marriage.

Michael suffered from bouts of depression because he was majoring in accounting when he really wanted to be an artist. He had hopes of driving around the country, visiting other artists, studying in a few studios, living in a small desert community. But he was on the fast track to working in a Big Six accounting firm because he knew his parents had spent their retirement savings on his education, and unless he got a good job, they would be bankrupt during their "golden years." As he said to me, "I know how hard they work to earn their money, and I have to make it up to them. They used to tell me, when I was a little kid, that they didn't care what I grew up to be, as long as I was happy. They don't say that anymore, because they know that being an artist would make me happy, but that's not realistic financially."

The End of Childhood Innocence

Think about all the exposure children get to today's problems. A friend of mine has a six-year-old daughter who was petrified on her first airplane flight—she had learned at school about the hole in the ozone layer and was worried that the plane would "fall into the hole and crash." Children hear constantly at school about environmental decay, contamination of the foods they eat, frightening strangers, as well as other concerns such as poverty, pollution, overpopulation, war, aging, disease, crime and violence, terrorism, and human-rights violations.

When we were children, we knew the boundaries of our neighborhoods, knew how far we could ride our bikes, knew which neighbors would invite us in for cookies and which would tell our parents if they saw us so much as thinking of riding, rather than walking, our bikes across an intersection. Today's children don't have such security. Many kids are in day care after school and rarely meet the other kids in their own neighborhoods. Parents today worry that children just hanging around the neighborhood are an invitation to trouble. We associate four or five kids leaning against a lamppost with gangs and problems, not with the carefree times of childhood.

Children are not encouraged to go to their neighbors' houses because we don't know our neighbors as well as we used to. When you and I were young, we probably had one man in the neighborhood who particularly liked children, who lifted us onto his lap and told us stories. Today we might worry that he is a child molester and report him to the police. With the horrible stories on television, wise parents can't help but be extremely cautious ... and that caution can't help but be transmitted unconsciously to their children as fear.

School Is Not the Haven It Once Was

A child's home away from home—school—is not the haven it once was, either. There are fewer and fewer opportunities for children to attend a nice, quiet, conservative school in which their biggest worry is whether they can copy their best friend's homework because they didn't finish their own. Many schools today have security guards and metal detectors at the doorways (and that includes elementary schools, not only high schools). Children are pressured to join gangs (or hang out with tougher, streetwise kids), and at a younger and younger age. Even so-called middle- and upper-class children are feeling the push to engage in activities their parents never dreamt of.

Remember those few bad boys who got a bad reputation for bragging about their promiscuous intentions in high school? Today, members of "sex posses" score points for having sex with as many girls as they can, regardless of the age of the girls. As early as middle school, both boys and girls now have to worry about the pressure to have sex, as well as the pressure to use alcohol and drugs. Even the smallest children worry about not fitting in without having the most expensive brand of sneakers ... and we have all heard the stories of children getting shot for their shoes ... and jackets ... and ...

Family Ties ... and Chains

We no longer think that home can or should match the ideal television family in which a mother wears high heels and pearls and hums merrily as she bakes cakes from scratch, where a father knows best, and where all problems are talked over and solved at the dinner table. Today we have a more realistic picture of the two-income family . . . or of the single parent who juggles work outside the home, housekeeping, and child care.

Still, home should be a place of safety and innocence. Problems arise when children have to become adults too quickly—a result of not feeling needed or wanted by parents, dealing with sexual harassment or abuse, or coping with being a pawn in a divorce or custody battle. Just being at home often demands a psychological hardiness that places enormous demands on children's emotional energies.

Living, loving, and working in today's world place demands on our emotional energies that require an enormous degree of psychological hardiness. Managing stress becomes a survival tool in more ways than one.

Perils of the Information Age

Ours is an Age of Information, with more information available to more people than ever before. With progress comes improved mass communication, meaning that vast amounts of information are given via television, radio, newspapers, and magazines. Much of that information naturally trickles down to children, who are exposed to more news about the world in a week of television than our grandparents were in their lifetimes. What effect does this have on the children? How has the Information Age transformed our children's experiences of childhood? What kinds of strains and stresses has it produced within them? And what does all this mean for us, the parents, who have an increased responsibility for keeping our children emotionally safe?

Are You a Family of Just Living Together?
The Information Age is also the Age of Technology. Although much of the technology of our age is useful, freeing up time for us to spend doing things we enjoy rather than drudge work, there can be a darker side to it. While family members may be living under one roof, there is no guarantee that they are interacting as a family. Each person may be individually involved in some electronic diversion—watching TV, playing video games, working on the computer. One characteristic of a healthy family is that its members communicate with each other; interaction satisfies their needs for belonging and acceptance. Because needs, interests, and concerns are shared, each member feels valued and loved.

Science has provided us with marvelous techniques for the dissemination of information via satellite, radio, television, movies, computers, and recordings, to name a few. Ultimately, this places vast amounts of information in the hands of almost everyone, quickly and efficiently. What happens in another region of the world airs on the six o'clock news in the home and is subject to our immediate reactions. Consider how events in Bosnia or Somalia (or a local event, for that matter) become the subject of conversations within minutes of their being relayed.

The Information Age pours vast amounts of information into our homes, imploding children's minds with dramatic images of the human condition from every corner of the world. How wonderful to be able to access information so quickly and efficiently. The question is, *are we guiding our children to understand what they see and hear and to develop healthy attitudes toward what they witness—some of which is beyond their ability to assimilate?* By the time they are ready for preschool, children today have seen an incredible amount of violence and sex on television. Television doesn't segregate its audience; it communicates the same information to everyone simultaneously, regardless of age or maturity level. Life in all its fullness is right up there on the screen for any wide-eyed child to view: madness, corruption, sadism, promiscuity, incest, and other topics of the Movie of the Week.

Just as the Information Age can provide wonderful and rich educational experiences for children, it can also have dire and disturbing consequences. Children soon learn that danger lurks everywhere: in the home, in the office, on the streets, at the playground.

Television Can Be an Unkind Babysitter

Next to the family, television is probably the most important influence on child development in our society. Children in the United States view an average of three to five hours of television daily. By high school graduation, the average kid will have spent more time in front of the television than in the classroom. Television informs us, entertains us, and keeps us company. It is also linked to violent or aggressive behavior, obesity, poor academic performance, precocious sexuality, and the use of drugs or alcohol in our children. It's becoming increasingly important that parents help their children use television as a positive, creative force and help them avoid television's negative influences.

Television exposes children to adult behaviors in ways that suggest that these behaviors are normal and risk-free. Sexual behavior and the use of alcohol or drugs are often portrayed in unrealistic or inviting terms. Because of the frequency with which these behaviors occur on television, the message seems to be that "everyone does it." Television characters rarely say no. Ten percent of adolescent girls in the United States get pregnant each year. The leading cause of death in teenage boys is accidents, 50 percent of which involve alcohol. Although television viewing is not the only way that children learn about sexuality and drug and alcohol use, the risks of these behaviors are not given equal time on television. The standards of sexuality on cable television are even more extreme.

In many households, TV has become the babysitter. It substitutes for conversation, for family interaction. And a violent babysitter it is. A 1982 report by the National Institute of Mental Health states that children who view more than two hours of television each day come to accept violent behavior as normal. When the television acts as a babysitter, children are both overwhelmed by the information they are getting and isolated within their electronic cocoon from other family members. It is part of our responsibility as parents to recognize both effects on our children and to understand how these effects can lead to increased stress and difficulties.

Violence on TV does lead to aggressive behavior from children and teenagers who watch, behavior that makes learning in school very difficult. Many of these children begin to see themselves as discipline problems and poor learners, and the cycle of low self-esteem begins.

Suggestions through Commercials

The average child sees more than 20,000 commercials during the 1,300 to 1,400 hours of television that he or she views annually. Advertisers spend roughly $700 million a year to make sure that their sales pitches reach large numbers of children.

Among the top TV advertisers are a number of corporations that aim all or most of their sales efforts at children.

Most food advertising aimed at children is for heavily sugared products such as candy and presweetened cereals. Commercials for meat, milk products, bread, and juice make up only about 4 percent of the food ads shown during "children's viewing time." This emphasis gives children a distorted picture of how they ought to eat. Ads that are often more entertaining than the programs themselves suggest that the way to eat is by snacking and eating sugary foods.

In prime-time television, eating is a frequent occurrence. The amount of TV that a child watches is directly related to the number of snacks a child eats and the types of foods chosen. It is therefore not surprising that a recent study found a direct relationship between the amount of television viewing and children's risk of obesity.

Tune In, Tune Out

What are the consequences of a young person's television viewing when he or she watches the plight of a man, woman, or child in war; sees nudity, violence, and family feuding in the next take; and then is offered the rude and arrogant Bart Simpson in the next? When children become intimate with all the horrors of the globe via TV, they need adults to help them understand what they see and what it means, to put these images into perspective. If not, the children will, over time, become numb to pain, hurt, injustice, and violence. By tuning in so frequently to television, they become overwhelmed with information, and eventually nothing they see on television seems real to them. Hitting someone over the head with a bottle is just fun, not injurious. Is it any wonder that we see an increase in young people acting out their frustration and anger toward each other, committing crimes and behaving without regard for the feelings of others? We must not underestimate the importance of helping our children gain an understanding of what they see on television. Without this guidance, a child may not hold to values that protect people nor feel compassion when others are in harm's way; most important, he or she may fail to be moved to act in a responsible way after witnessing something that requires action.

How to Use the Information Age to Your Advantage

As parents, we need to understand the prominence of mass communication in our children's lives. The television and radio and newspaper are not going to go away; our children are not going to ignore them. Even children who aren't sitting in front of the television for three or four hours a day hear the reports of the latest shows from their friends. We need to be certain that we give our children the skills to place what they hear and see and learn into perspective. We need to help them develop common-sense values. Here are some ways to deal with the stress and strains of the information age.

1. Encourage questions. One of the best things we can do is to let our children know we are always willing to answer questions. Children need to know that they can ask us to explain things, that we will be willing to take the time to answer their questions without judging them as "dumb" or ridiculous.

2. Recognize confusion and fears in the patterns of questions and comments. The more you let your children talk, the more you can recognize a pattern. If your fifteen-year-old constantly asks you whether you have locked the garage door, checked the windows, put the dog out in the yard, you might sense an uneasiness about personal safety, possibly from watching television shows about break-ins and burglaries. If your five-year-old screams when she sees you tap a newspaper on your dog's nose for piddling on the carpet, it may be because she fears the dog will turn into a horror-movie beast and attack you. Listen as your children talk; try to hear what is behind their comments and questions so you know where to begin to provide support and help.

3. Talk about what your children are seeing. When you watch a show with your children, point out the moral of the story. Hollywood still ends most shows with the bad guys getting their comeuppance. Emphasize that actions have consequences. For example, if a scene emphasizes or implies the characters are having sex, you might use this as an opportunity to talk about the importance of safe sex.

4. Inject a note of reality. When a safe falls on a cartoon character's head, he is not hurt. He flattens out, turns into a hubcap, rolls down a hill, then pops back up into his original form. Your small children will naturally get a big kick out of this. However, you might remind them that in real life, getting hit, or having something fall on them, hurts like mad. Bring up a real-life situation: "Remember when you dropped your book on your toe and you limped around all evening? Imagine how much a safe would hurt! No one could get up after that." Such comments are especially important about guns and knives. Children need to recognize the real-life consequences of actions.

5. Teach your children that actions have consequences. Most news reports and TV shows have good guys and bad guys. Even very young children recognize that bad guys behave differently from good guys. A friend of mine with a four-year-old teaches values by playing a good guy/bad guy game. She mentions an action, then her son has to shout out whether it's something a good guy or a bad guy would do. For example, she says, "breaking a window," and Trevor responds, "bad guy!" As Trev gets older, my friend might add punishments and rewards to the game. For example, she could say, "breaking a window," and expect Trev to say, "must pay for the window." An action like stealing a car would bring the response "arrested by the police." The goal is to make certain your children make the connection between proper actions and their rewards and improper actions and their penalties. This is especially important these days when children see that the bad guys seem to be doing better than the good guys: Drug dealers drive expensive cars, dress in the latest fashions, and frequent the best and most expensive restaurants.

6. Emphasize the safety of your home. Young children especially, but older children as well, worry that things that they see on television could happen to them. On the five o'clock news they see a clean-cut man being led away in handcuffs for embezzlement and wonder whether someone will come to take away their own daddy. Encourage your children to talk about their fears. Don't immediately pooh-pooh them, saying they will never happen. Kids know that these things can in fact occur. Maybe your daughter's best friend's father was robbed and beaten. If it happened to her friend's dad, she reasons, why couldn't it happen to her own? Talk about what you would do if it ever did happen. Let your children know what you do to ensure your and their safety.

7. Emphasize the differences between your children's lives and what is shown on the screen. When you see your child watching a show in which a robber breaks into a house, let him help you lock up in the evening and see how the deadbolts and window locks work. Keep letting your children see that what they watch on television does not mirror their life, that their home is different from the house of the robbery victim on television.

8. Limit your child's television viewing. Note how many hours of television your children watch—you will probably need to limit them. You should also guide what your children watch. Hang tough! Remember that before television, families had no trouble finding other ways to inform and entertain themselves.

It can be difficult for parents to effectively monitor and control the amount of television their children watch. "Lock out" devices are available so that certain channels, such as pornographic channels on cable television, cannot be seen. Another helpful tool is an electronic device called Supervision that allows parents to automatically regulate the amount of television their children watch. This device and other similar ones allow parents to create flexible and tailored viewing guidelines. For example, you may have a child who does not need daily scheduled viewing times but does need a daily time allowance. In this case the child would be allowed to watch any time of day but would not be able to exceed his or her daily viewing allowance. Or you may want to set up the daily scheduled viewing so that there is no television after 9:00 P.M. Such monitoring not only solves the problem of unchecked and excessive television viewing but teaches your children to budget their viewing time and to select quality programming instead of spending mindless hours in front of the TV.

These devices can also be employed to limit the use of video games (such as Nintendo and Sega) and VCRs as well. If you have videotapes in your home library that are not suitable for viewing by younger children, or if you are concerned that your child may rent and view an inappropriate tape while you are not present, then you can block the VCR's use until you are present.

Sharing More Than an Address
When television is a big part of a child's life and then is cut back, the child is going to complain. Stand your ground. And give your child plenty of attention, especially in the form of communication. Now that the television is turned off, you have time to talk. Ask your children how their day has gone. Go over their homework. Play board games, involve them in household

chores and meal preparation, take walks, work out together. During each of these activities, you have the opportunity to share thoughts. Communicating is about connecting. Parents and children can communicate with small talk about the events of the day, through giggling over something silly, by making faces together over dinner. The point is, a family is more than just people who live in the same home; it is people who share and help each other in their journeys—physically, emotionally, mentally, spiritually. What your child learns about family becomes an important foundation of his or her values.

There's no need to cut out television viewing entirely, of course, but monitor it so that you know your children are able to understand what they are watching. Discuss the television shows, along with anything else your children want to talk about. And communicate in words. Family ties nurture children in times of stress.

Is Childhood Disappearing?
The Perils of a Hurried-Up World

We live in a revved-up, fast-paced world of constant change. We've moved from being a stationary culture (our grandparents rarely moved from city to city, and almost never from state to state; many of them lived their entire lives within a five-mile radius) to being a very mobile one (just think of how many times you have moved, and whether any of your neighbors have been around for more than a few years). Time is of the essence. Being on time, meeting a deadline, matters more and more. Overnight delivery services have boomed in the past decade. Faxes take over when overnight is too long. Aboard the Concorde you can fly from New York to Paris in a mere four hours. We tap our feet and hum impatiently when a telephone call takes more than a few seconds to connect.

Today we are living in the midst of a vast and profound revolution creating stress and pressures that are quite different from those experienced even a decade ago. The shift from a manufacturing society to an information society is magnified and accelerated by continual scientific and technological breakthroughs, and characterized by rapid change and increasing choices and options. All this requires special adaptive coping skills.

Not only are we involved in more change, but the *pace* of change is accelerating. As Alvin Toffler so aptly described years ago in his blockbuster book, *Future Shock*, these changes can dramatically affect how and where we live and work. An increase in the rate of change affects our adaptation to new conveniences and can erode our sense of permanence and stability, depriving us of a feeling of real accomplishment.

Today's child has become the unwilling, unintended victim of constantly being hurried. Harried as so many of today's parents are, it is often easier to tie a child's shoelaces than to wait while she ties them herself. It's often faster to tidy up your youngster's room than to make the necessary effort to see that he keeps it clean himself. It is easier to hand a child lunch money than to have her make her own lunch. Pulling on your four-year-old's T-shirt is quicker than waiting for him to get it on himself, especially when you need to get ready to go off to work. Setting the table yourself is less trouble than taking the time to supervise a young child doing that task, especially when you want to get to your briefcase of work waiting for you. It's much easier to collect the crayons and coloring book from the dining room table than it is to see that your child does it herself, especially if it turns the limited time you have together into a complaint-filled evening. It's easier to whip through a page or two of your second-grade child's math homework than it is to tutor and supervise that child's painstaking efforts at completing those problems for himself.

Hurried parents rush through tasks and produce a harried child who gets the message that faster is better, feels helpless because he can't keep up, and is pressured too soon to grow up.

Children have always been in a hurry to grow up; this is nothing new. It's cute to see small children dressed in Mommy's clothing or wearing Daddy's oversized shoes. But there is a difference between wanting to grow up—a normal, healthy part of childhood—and having grown-up concerns forced upon one.

Rushing children and rushing childhood have consequences. We are now witnessing an erasure of the dividing line between childhood and adulthood and a blurring of childlike and adult behaviors. Children commit crimes once attributed to adults and are tried as adults more and more frequently. Children have many of the same legal rights as adults and a growing list of responsibilities to go with those rights. Children's games are rapidly disappearing, replaced by organized sports that are more and more competitive. Play for play's sake is gone; now all games and toys must have an educational purpose. Whatever happened to the *fun* of just being a child? Today's child is often forced to assume the physical, psychological, and social trappings of adulthood before he or she is prepared to do so. Today's world is such that even very young children are taught sex education and how to prevent sexually transmitted diseases for their own safety. Toddlers are taught to dial 911 and how to recognize improper touching.

Why should we be concerned if children have fewer opportunities to experience childhood? Because premature adulthood has its problems. It forces the child to leapfrog the activities of childhood that prepare him for adulthood, and to play adult games for which he is ill prepared. Expecting a child to be a smaller version of an adult who needs minimal direction and support, to metamorphose instantly into maturity, can impair a child's ability to construct a secure personal identity, to develop feelings of belonging and a respect for limits, leaving him more vulnerable and less competent to meet the challenges that are inevitable in life. Such children, often jaded by their midteens, are unable to cope with the problems facing them. Children who are confused and lack clear moral standards become alienated and feel outside of society rather than a part of it. They are more likely to fall prey to the hazards of low self-esteem—such as dependency, addictions, and the like. A lack of childhood sends out ripple effects that reach beyond the child to his family, neighborhood, and society at large.

Stress for Success—Pushing to Find Our Children's Potential
When we think back on our childhood, we remember how time seemed to drag. Summers went on forever. The week before Christmas seemed like a year. We had few obligations beyond our chores and our homework. Time was much less of a concern to us than finding the best place to ride our bikes or teasing our younger sister. But nowadays, children's lives are so scheduled that the days seem to fly by. They are just as likely as adults to

say, "I don't know where the time went!" One of the reasons for this is the pressure that parents put on their children to live up to their potential by spending every possible minute searching for what they are good at. Success seems to be achieved at a much earlier age than it used to be. Announcers at sports events delight in telling their audiences that this twelve-year-old gymnast is the youngest Olympian ever, or that this tennis player made the Wimbledon semifinals at age fifteen. Parents hear these announcements and push their children even harder to succeed. Children no longer have the luxury of time to "find themselves"; they have their parents pushing them constantly.

Six-year-old Cris has a twelve-year-old brother, Ron, whom he adores. Ron is on the swim team, earns money by taking care of some of the neighborhood dogs, and is very active. Cris wants to be just like him. Cris's parents encourage this because when the two boys are together, their parents know where they are, can allot only one parent for supervision, and don't have to make two round trips transporting them. Therefore, Cris is taking swimming lessons on Mondays and Fridays. When his brother walks the dogs every afternoon, Cris goes along, taking large steps to try to keep up with his brother. His parents tell Cris that he has to go, since neither of them will be home to take care of him. Most of the time he enjoys being around Ron and the dogs, but sometimes he is just too tired. Ron is good on the computer, so Cris takes a special beginner computer class Tuesdays and Thursdays after school. On Wednesdays, Cris participates in a Seniors and Children project, in which "grandmothers" and "grandfathers" in nursing homes meet with young children. On Saturday and Sunday Cris goes to visit his father, who is divorced from Cris's mother and lives on the other side of the city. The father is so eager to spend time with his son that he schedules every minute. Since Cris showed some interest in watching his father play tennis, he and his dad now go to beginner tennis classes. They also go to concerts, and Cris's dad just bought a small keyboard, which he is trying to teach Cris to play.

Swimming, dog walking, learning about computers, visiting senior citizens, traveling to see Dad, tennis lessons, music lessons: Cris doesn't have a minute to call his own. His parents are not trying to push him but to keep him busy and occupied, and, of course, to help him "develop his potential." He enjoys the individual activities, but there are times when they all get to be too much for him. That's when he just wants to sit in front of the TV, or to read a book, or merely to sit in the front yard and do absolutely nothing. He has a lot of friends, but when they're together they're usually in school or taking some sort of lesson, where they're supposed to be quiet and pay attention.

Cris's parents mean well, but they are pushing too hard. We adults think children have boundless energy because they always seem to be in motion. But children have their limits, too. Pushing our children to achieve too much (and at an early age) can cause them to burn out. If we keep pushing and pushing, something has to give. Unfortunately, that something is usually physical or mental or emotional health.

Are You Pushing Your Child Too Hard?
A Checklist

It's important to let children be children, to have "downtime." Children sometimes need to shut down to prevent overload. Here's a checklist you can use to detect whether you are pushing your children too hard.

1. How many hours a day does your child spend in downtime? Like busy adults, children, too, need time to relax and time to play.

2. How many hours a week are devoted to extracurricular lessons of any sort, including sports? If the child has two hours or more every single day, including weekends, he is probably overscheduled. There are exceptions, of course; for instance, during football season there may be daily practices. But when football season turns into basketball season turns into baseball season, with no time off between sports, your child may feel overwhelmed. This is true not only for older children but for very young children as well: The child going from grade school to tutoring labs to tumbling classes gets overwhelmed, too.

3. Does your child eat most of his meals at home, or does he eat at the day-care center, at the babysitter's home, at school, at fast-food restaurants on the way to or from somewhere, at friends' houses? Mealtimes at home are good times for children to lean back, relax, and chat about the little things. Small talk can be very soothing.

4. Does your child have trouble remembering all the activities he is in, or what activity is scheduled for what day? Most children enjoy their activities so much that each one stands out like a separate jewel. When they all begin to run together, the child is probably doing too much.

5. Does your child have adequate time for fellowship and informal socializing with others? Is there time for play and fun? How much time does your older child have for talking on the telephone with friends? A child whose schedule doesn't allow for time with friends except in the course of "doing something" doesn't have enough unscheduled time.

6. What hobbies does your child have at home? What projects has he started at home? Most children go through a phase when they treasure a book or stamp collection, or build models, or rearrange their bedrooms. If your child doesn't do any of these things at home, he might not be home enough to feel comfortable starting a project there.

Children Need Stability

As any parent who has read the same bedtime story over and over to a child knows, children need stability. They like to hear the same tales, wear the same clothes, do the same things. They become upset and stressed if things are different. It's not only small children who like this consistency. Which of us hasn't been yelled at for laundering or—worse yet!—throwing out a favorite pair of sweat socks that were host to a hundred holes? Everyone from a small child to a teenager has certain items that are sacred, that must never be tossed out. Teenagers, who think they are so creative and original and different, are notorious for liking rituals. They see the same friends, call each other at the same times, hang out at the same places. They need continuity in their lives to feel comfortable.

Think back to when you were a child and your family moved. Wasn't it terrifying to meet new people, to find a new clique to fit into at school? You weren't sure how to dress, whether you would know the latest dances, what topics to talk about. In times of larger families, children had at least one sibling they could commiserate with and draw strength from. Today there are very many one-child families, leaving many children without a sibling to go through all the changes with.

Developing Stability

What can you do to provide more stability in your children's lives? Obviously, some things are tougher to control than others—such as having to move to a new job, or remarrying and providing your child with new stepsiblings. Here are suggestions to provide continuity for your children:

1. Leave room in the schedule for downtime. Evaluate your children's schedules. Is your child complaining about not having enough time to do what he or she wants to do? If so, one activity can be scaled down or removed to provide more time for relaxation. Not all quiet time is wasted time.

2. Set aside "us" time. Children want to be special, to be your favorite, no matter how many siblings they have. For each child, set aside time each week to spend with that child and that child alone. You can take a walk, go to the park, sit and read, whatever, as long as it's just the two of you. Make every effort to continue this tradition, to let your child know that even if your family moves or increases or the situation around him changes in some other way, your special time will remain.

3. Ask your children what they want to do. It's surprising how often we forget to do this simple thing. Even small children are relatively vocal when it comes to saying what they like and dislike. Ask your children whether they would like to go to the swimming pool; don't immediately assume that doing so is a big treat for them just because you loved going when you were a child. Maybe they liked going to the pool last year but now would rather stay home and play with their dog.

4. Prepare your children for the inevitability of some changes. All children will *have* to deal with some changes at some times in their lives. Parents need to discuss the possibility of changes and show children that change is normal and can be enjoyed rather than feared. For example, a parent might talk to her children about their oldest sibling's going off to school and not living at home anymore. To a small child, this "loss" of a sibling is traumatic. If she is aware this is going to happen, she can develop strategies for coping with the change. Older children need to know that changes in their lives do not mean that you will no longer be there for them. Even a child who is away at college or has her own apartment needs a secure home base. How far in advance you prepare your child for an upcoming change varies according to your child's age, personality, and ability to handle the consequences of the change. For example, if the family pet's health is so poor that it must be put to sleep, you probably have some idea of how traumatic that will be for your child. Each family member will mourn the loss of the pet according to his or her ability to understand the circumstances that surround the problem. (Has the pet been ill for some time, or is this a new and urgent condition?) Helping your child cope with the stress of change depends on your deepening his or her understanding of what must be done, tempered by helping the child overcome the feeling of loss over time. (Will you replace the pet with a new one?) Every child's personality is different, and you know better than anyone what your child can manage. The goal is to provide stability, a still center, while acknowledging that change will occur.

Can we grasp the full significance of living in a world of such rapid change and its effects on our children? Probably not. This is even more reason to help our children learn skills to manage the stress that is sure to be a part of their lives. The next chapter helps parents examine how children experience responsibility and decision making, and shows parents how they can help children develop the skills to minimize the stress of living in a "brave new world."

Chapter 2

RESPONSIBILITY, DECISION MAKING, AND STRESS

When I was small, my classmates and I would drop our pennies in the Red Cross bucket that made the rounds of the classroom, get a little tin pin that folded over the collar of our shirts, and feel that we had done our part to feed the hungry children in China or India or wherever. That was pretty much the extent of our social responsibility until we grew up and began allocating money from our paychecks to the United Fund, feeling we had helped to clothe the homeless, to provide disaster relief funds, and, again, "whatever." Many of us probably wish we had more time or money to do more for our fellow human beings, but for the most part, we leave altruism to the Other Guy or to the Mother Teresas of the world.

Children today don't wear the blinders that we wore. The Information Age makes them very aware of the gaps in justice and equality. We of course heard stories about the poverty in nebulous "third-world countries," but we didn't see the pictures as our children do today, and we didn't understand these conditions and their implications with the depth and magnitude that our children do. We might have donated our old clothes to the less fortunate, but we never actually came into contact with them. Our children now take field trips to soup kitchens to help feed the poor. They go to inner-city churches at Christmas and donate toys for children. When my daughter was a sophomore in high school her class adopted an overseas family and communicated with them by letter and telephone. By the time she was a senior, her class had sponsored them to come live in America, assisting this family in everything from raising funds for the plane trip to America, to finding shelter, providing food and clothes, and arranging jobs for the parents. The class also helped the three children adjust to the local schools, providing big brother and big sister friendship and support and tutoring the children and parents in English. That's a very different sort of participation in the responsibility of caring for our fellow man.

My Brother's Keeper . . . And My Sister's . . . And the Planet's

Today children know much more about the world at large than we did. As our society has become more global, we have learned that we truly are responsible for the welfare of those far away. When our sprays deplete the ozone layer, people in Patagonia can't go out in the noonday sun. When our tankers cause an oil spill in the far north, fishermen can't make a living for months, even years.

While this new awareness of social responsibility is a large leap forward toward a more sensitive, caring, compassionate society, it can also create stress for children. Most children are basically idealists. They see themselves on white chargers, rushing to rescue those in need. Every day they hear at school about other cultures, other races, other socioeconomic strata. The first stress begins when they learn that there are so many problems in the world. Children are aware that the world is full of want, of hunger, of pain, of suffering. They don't know what to do to make these conditions go away, yet they would like to. When they see on television that thousands of people have died from starvation in Africa, they know that shipping their leftover pizza to Somalia is not going to solve the problem. Older children know that no one seems to be accomplishing very much, and they wonder if adults have their priorities in order. When my daughter's class undertook the project to help the overseas family immigrate to America, they ran into bureaucratic delays that to them were needless and senseless; they couldn't understand why helping out couldn't be easier than it was. Children think it's crazy that we can build another bomber plane but can't save the lives of starving children. They feel powerless; it is unlikely that they can convince the government to reroute the funds to the children. Children are quite different from adults in the way they see problems and their resolutions.

Children Personalize World Problems
Children also experience stress when they begin to personalize world problems. For example, six-year-old Tim came home one

day and announced to his mother that he thought it a good idea to buy a Nintendo program for the school toy drive. When his mother explained that none of the children who would be getting the toys would have a Nintendo machine to play the game on, Tim was shocked. After all, *everyone* had a Nintendo machine, even the little nerdy kids. Status in his small world was based on having the most games, the latest and the best games. Tim couldn't imagine a world in which there was absolutely no Nintendo. Then, as he thought about it more, he began to worry that someday *he* could be Nintendo-less. Being a smart child, he realized that if other children were without the things he took for granted, he might someday be without them, too.

While we adults think of childhood as a time when we protect our children, most kids are worldly enough to realize that even the strongest daddy or smartest mommy might get fired, and that even the best parents can't protect them from getting cancer. They watch the news and see that formerly middle-class families are now homeless, as parents lose their long-term jobs in factories and offices. Can we really be surprised when they wonder whether these things could happen to them? Children hear adults discuss their worries about the economy, about possible downsizing at work and elimination of jobs; children sense these fears and internalize them as a world filled with uncertainty and, worse, strife.

There is also a "reverse stress" that can occur when children become aware of the problems of the world. They might feel guilty and ashamed of themselves for not caring *more*. As fifteen-year-old Amanda told me, "I know that I should be doing more to help the environment. My friends are all going door-to-door to pick up cans and glass for recycling this weekend. But I don't want to spend my weekend like that. I'd rather clean my room and rearrange my closet, or go to the movies or the mall with my girlfriend. That probably means that I'm not very socially conscious or that I'm not 'politically correct,' doesn't it?" There is so much on the news these days about social responsibility that children feel pressure to take a stance. They know they "should" do this and "should" do that to help.

Racism, Children, and Stress

Just as adults constantly grapple with learning to respect, appreciate, and utilize diversity in their work, it is a task that more and more children are confronting in school and in their neighborhoods. For the past two years, eleven-year-old Maria has been bused to a school in an all-white suburb. She is one of about twenty Hispanic students. Maria has always felt accepted by the other students because she is friendly and bright. But this year, black students were bused to the school. When Maria made friends with Janetta, who sat next to her in music class, her Caucasian friends began taunting her. Although Maria tried to make Janetta a part of the group, her girlfriends said Maria had to make a choice between Janetta and them. She chose to remain with her white friends and tried to ignore their snide comments about Janetta. It didn't make sense to Maria that her friends would ask her to choose between them and Janetta. It occurred to Maria that if she couldn't stop racism in her little group, it might be impossible to change it in the world.

Maria was surprised to find that her friends were racist, because they hadn't been to her. When she questioned them about it, they said that Maria wasn't all *that* Hispanic, that she was light skinned and didn't have an accent, so she was "almost white." When Maria realized how much racism there was in the world, she was very disappointed. She had been taught that everyone had the same opportunities, but she realized it wasn't so.

How Much Responsibility Is Too Much?

Some children internalize the world's problems and feel a strong sense of responsibility to solve them. Others can't begin to grasp them, while others are overwhelmed by them. Where in this range do your children fall? Listen to your children when they talk about problems. You are accustomed to listening closely when they talk about personal problems, ranging from their ABCs to bad hair days, but can you identify what they feel about the larger picture? Ask your children what they feel about the fact that the environment is polluted, that species of animals are becoming extinct every year, that drug abuse is on the rise. Even small children can have some feelings for the state of the world, the state of society.

Are your children doing anything to help, and if so, how seriously do they take their activities? If your fifteen-year-old daughter is going to pick up trash at the beach, is it because she cares about pollution or because she wants to meet the boys who will be there? Does your eight-year-old who wears a JUST SAY NO TO DRUGS T-shirt care about spreading the message, or does he just think the shirt is cool? Talk with your children about topics like poverty, sexism, and world peace. Find out what they think about these conditions, and how they feel they can be personally and socially responsible in helping to make the world a better place for all.

Keeping Perspective

What can parents do to help their children develop a sense of responsibility without being overwhelmed by the problems of the world? Here's a framework to help you begin:

1. Be honest and realistic. Don't automatically tell your children that the problem isn't as bad as they thought or that it will go away soon. Something like global pollution or racism is probably not going to be solved in our children's lifetimes, unfortunately. Help your children understand the problem clearly and, depending upon the age and emotional stability of your child, talk about ways she or he can realistically become a part of the solution.

2. Don't belittle your children's social concerns. Even if you think it is funny that your seven-year-old is very upset about the possible extinction of the pygmy hippopotamus, don't mock his concerns. Talk to your children and hear their fears and concerns. Whether or not you agree with them, these problems are very real to your children. Just talking about their concerns can help them decide what, if anything, they can do to help eradicate or resolve a particular social problem.

3. Help your children feel their efforts are worthwhile. Children think that if they use an environmentally incorrect shampoo they might be directly responsible for polluting the ocean and causing the death of microscopic marine life. You don't want them to think that it's of no use even to try to solve a problem that is grand in scope. Help them see that there are many people all over the world who have contributed to the problem and are working toward a solution. Tell your children that every little bit helps, that recycling cans is important even if the household next door refuses to do so. Show them that problems such as racism and sexism get just a little bit better each time they treat a person as a human being, not as a stereotype. If feasible, keep records of what they and their friends have done, and how it has helped. For example, have them contribute to a fund for a city playground, then take them there once the playground is built and show them how children are having fun, due at least in part to them.

4. Value your child's priorities. While you may think the most important issue facing America today is literacy and education, your teenage son might think it is overhauling the legal profession. While you may think that government funds should be directed toward defensive military weapons, your daughter might think they should go toward hot lunch programs in the schools. Talk with your children about why they feel as they do, about what has influenced their point of view. Do this without negating their sense of what is important, and why. Then agree to disagree. It's okay if you have different priorities. The important thing is that your children learn to get involved, to think about what is going on in the world, to formulate a sense of right and wrong about it, and to consider how they might contribute to the well-being of all.

5. Praise your child's sense of moral responsibility. Let your children know that you are proud of their sense of moral responsibility. In order for our children to become socially responsible, they must have a sense of moral and ethical accountability—to their friends, to their society, to the planet. Our goal as parents is to foster that responsibility while not projecting the magnitude of the problem to the point where it becomes so overwhelming that children feel it is impossible to impact it in any useful way.

6. Recognize when your child's sense of responsibility is beginning to cause stress. Look for signs that your children are taking too many problems on, that they are too involved in trying to cure the world's every ailment. Identify the severity of the stress: Will this overwhelming sense of responsibility pass as the children move on to new interests, or is it deeply felt? What is the cause of the stress? If your children saw a homeless person on their way to school, or heard a lecture about the environment, they may be particularly interested for only that day, or their interest may linger. Does your son constantly talk about the homeless person he saw? Is your daughter frightened by what she heard about the environment, or having nightmares about it? Watch for signs that your child is overly involved to the point of experiencing ongoing distress.

7. Help your children understand their role. Children often feel as if everything is their fault. We all know that when a marriage breaks up, children frequently think that it is because of something they said or did. Children are quick to personalize things. It is easy, then, for children to believe that the problems of the world are somehow their fault as well. While we smile over the story of the seven-year-old boy who says he doesn't want to take a bath and waste water during a drought, some children do think that only they can solve the woes of the world. Help your children put things in perspective, showing them that they are not the sole cause of the problem but that they can make a difference when they are aware of the problem. For example, tell your sixteen-year-old that she doesn't pollute the globe just by driving around in her old car but that she does have a responsibility to keep it tuned up so that it will pollute just a little bit less.

8. Recognize the importance of a sense of social responsibility. We need to recognize that by having a sense of social responsibility, our children help themselves as well as society. We need to raise our children with a broader approach to what a "family" is. If the family becomes a unit, entire of itself, romanticized, idealized, we begin to care less about the community and become less involved with those outside our immediate family units. We need a way to show love, to accept mutual obligation and interdependence, that goes beyond our immediate family to the community at large.

Correcting the Stress of Social Ills

Some social problems have been around as long as humankind (poverty, disease); new ones seem to be born every generation (pollution, the demise of the rain forest). Children are our best hope for solving those problems and thus, naturally, must be taught about them. We must instill in them a sense of responsibility for working toward solutions. However, the problems of the world should not be placed solely upon the shoulders of a child. When your children are so involved in social problems as to be stressed over them, help them:

- identify the immediate sources of their stress (did they see a TV show on poverty? was there a guest speaker at school?);
- recognize the severity of the stress (will it pass as the children move on to a new interest, or is it something more deeply felt?);
- understand their role in solving social problems (they are responsible neither for the creation of the problem nor exclusively for the solution of it);
- feel empowered (they can be doing something productive to help, even if it seems like a very little bit).

Finally, stresses of this nature can be reduced greatly in our children when we simply reassure them that we understand their concerns, that we respect them for their caring, and that we support them in their efforts.

Teaching Your Child to Accept Responsibility

Ask a small child what responsibility means and she will probably rattle off a list of chores that you have assigned her: walk the dog, dust the living room table, make her bed. An older child might give a broader definition: keep your word, do what you said you would, make sure other people can rely on you. While responsibility means different things to children of different ages, we parents work very hard to rear responsible children.

We want our children to understand the importance of behaving responsibly and the repercussions of irresponsible actions. Yet sometimes this responsibility can be overwhelming to children and be yet another stressor in their lives. How can we find a balance, teaching our children to behave responsibly but not making them feel they have too many burdens?

Before you begin teaching your children responsibility, be certain you have the concept clear in your own mind. What does responsibility mean to you? What responsibilities do you think children should have, and at what ages? Most parents feel that basic responsibilities include keeping a clean room and picking up any mess made in other rooms of the house. When our children become students we want them to meet the requirements of being a learner and to do their homework religiously. Another responsibility is for personal hygiene, being bathed and combed and well dressed. There is financial responsibility, in which children learn to budget and to spend wisely their allowances or income from part-time jobs. Children need to become responsible with their time, getting to school before the bell rings, keeping curfew, managing to fit in all their activities and still have downtime left.

Like all parents, you want your children to be responsible people, but *what* do you want them to be responsible for doing? Sometimes I ask parents to tell me specifically what they have told their children about being responsible—what they are to do, and the consequences of not following through. Often I learn not only that parents haven't given their children any such guidelines but that in many cases the parents haven't even developed one themselves. We often grumble to ourselves that our spouses or bosses expect us to be mind readers, but we still expect our children to have that power. Children do not know what they are supposed to do nor what the standards are for acceptable performance unless they are told and shown how it is to be done. It must first be clear in the parent's mind. Articulate for your children what they are to do and what the standards are for acceptable performance.

Responsibility in the Family

Chances are you learned to be a responsible person under a set of conditions very different from today's. The world has changed so much since we were young that the same rules may not apply. For example, in my own childhood, I had morning and evening chores on the farm and had to care for five siblings. I wasn't always happy about what I had to do, but I knew I was needed. Nowadays children don't have that same sense of being needed; in fact, many of them consider that they are doing their parents a personal favor when they so much as make their beds!

Children learn responsibility best in the context of family life. It used to be that several generations of the same family lived and worked together. Everyone was responsible for taking care of the young and the old, for working in the family business. Today, families are more isolated. The grandparents live on their own or in custodial facilities. Parents go off to work, leaving children to spend more time on their own, with less parental guidance and fewer guidelines and opportunities for developing personal and family responsibilities. Children are expected to become responsible without having sufficient guidance in learning how to be so. Too much is demanded of them without enough instruction, a sure recipe for stress.

In a study spanning twenty years, psychologist Emmy Werner

attempted to identify some of the individual, family, and cultural factors that increase or decrease a child's risk of developing serious problems in life. Werner and a team of physicians, nurses, social workers, and psychologists followed the development of nearly a thousand children of divorced or troubled parents. One-third of the children in the study experienced a difficult and turbulent adolescence. While some of the children got into serious trouble, the majority did not. Of the children who did not get into trouble, the most striking characteristic that emerged was that they had caregiving responsibilities for fellow family members. They were in charge of helping others. The feeling of being needed, and the emotional support they received, were major protective factors in the midst of chronic poverty and/or serious family disruptions.

Other studies show similar results. A long-term Harvard study yielded startling information about how to raise happy, stress-free children. Begun forty years ago in an effort to understand juvenile delinquency, the study followed the lives of nearly five hundred teenagers, many from impoverished or broken homes. When the subjects were compared at middle age, one fact stood out: Regardless of intelligence, family income, ethnic background, or amount of education, those who had responsibilities in shared home and work projects as children, even if this meant only simple household chores, enjoyed happier and more productive lives than those who had no such responsibilities. They had better marriages, closer relationships with their children, and greater job satisfaction. They were healthier and lived longer. Above all, they were happier.

Ground Rules for Teaching Responsibility

Responsibility can be a benefit or a bane. How can we identify that fine line between the two, to keep from crossing over it? How can we instill responsibility in our children while not creating stress?

1. Start early. Begin teaching responsibility to your children when they are young. Your two-year-old might be expected to put her toys away. Ask a three-year-old to put out the napkins when the table is set; a four-year-old can put out the silverware. There are no hard and fast rules about what your children should do at different ages. When assigning chores and responsibilities, keep your children's strengths and weaknesses in mind. If your child is clumsy, making her put the china and crystal on the table provides a greater lesson in stress than in responsibility. Surely she can do something else, like fold the laundry, in which dropping things won't matter so much. Be certain your children are capable of doing what you expect them to do.

If you haven't expected anything of your child but decide to now, begin with simple tasks and gradually increase his responsibilities. If you suddenly tell a carefree twelve-year-old that he is old enough to start assuming responsibilities, he will no doubt fight you on it, having never had to do anything before. Start out with one or two tasks and then increase your demands as your child develops a habit of doing what you expect.

2. Make your expectations clear, predictable, and reasonable. Be certain in your own mind what you want your children to do. Write down their responsibilities; discuss them with your children for as long as it takes them to understand. If your child has failed to live up to previous responsibilities, take the time to explain exactly what he or she did wrong and then provide suggestions on how to do better this time. Make sure that you have shown him exactly how to do the task, and assist him in the task until he can do it on his own. Perhaps you have asked your five-year-old to fold his clothes and put them neatly in his drawer and then you discover that he has simply crammed the clothes unfolded into the drawer. Rather than saying, "You know that's not how you should do it. Do it again," you might say, "Your clothes are not folded neatly, as they must be. Would you like me to stay here in your room until you fold them, or would you like me to come back in a few minutes and check on them?" If you feel that your child has not yet mastered how to fold clothes correctly so that they fit in the drawer (a common problem for a five-year-old), then help your child fold them, once again teaching and reinforcing the skill. Do this good-naturedly; remember that you are modeling an attitude as much as a skill. Don't use put-downs that tear down. Tearing down your child only creates stress for both of you. Your child knows you are disappointed. She may feel that since she is bound to let you down no matter what she does, why even try to do better? And don't do the task yourself while your child looks on or goes out to play. Doing the task yourself only teaches your child that you are trainable and that he can get out of the responsibility.

3. Specify the consequence ahead of time. Children need to know that you have already decided what the consequence will be if they don't assume their responsibilities. Set your standards and discuss fully what will happen if they are not met. "Rick, I expect you to walk the dog every afternoon after school. There will be no television or Nintendo games until this is done." When children know exactly what will happen, they are more likely not only to assume responsibility for doing the task, but to acknowledge and accept the consequence of not doing so.

Few parents would disagree that it is a pleasure to have a child who is willing and able to assume responsibility for what is expected of him. Teach your children to be responsible people, personally and socially and in ways that are both reasonable and realistic. Children learn to be responsible when parents teach children that being responsible is a virtue.

Teaching Your Child to Make Good Decisions

The information explosion means more options and opportunities than ever before; your children will need to make many decisions, and wise decisions at that. Today's child needs excellent skills in identifying a wide array of options and in evaluating the consequences of his decisions. After all, the better the decision, the less stress. The young person who makes poor decisions contributes to his stress level.

To Thine Own Self Be True

The most common question asked of a child is "What do you want to be when you grow up?" We are accustomed to hearing children tell us they want to be astronauts, teachers, engineers, basketball players, physical therapists, doctors, bankers, actors, computer programmers, lawyers. The most common question asked of adults in a social setting is "What do you do?" It seems that we begin even as children to define ourselves by our work and careers. If you were to answer the question with a big smile and the comment "I strive to be happy and personally fulfilled in every aspect of my life, from family to work to friends," you would undoubtedly get many strange looks. Talking about personal enrichment just isn't done. But things are changing.

Increasing numbers of us are seeing that there is more to life than just work, more to life than the leisure hours we fill with play that seems like work: competitive racquetball, reading groups, continuing-education classes. It's no surprise that self-help books are selling well, that courses in getting to know yourself are sold out. Our parents and grandparents were so busy building careers and taking care of their families that they rarely had time to take care of themselves, especially that inner self that needs so much nurturing. We are only now beginning to overcome the ethics of self-denial and sacrifice, to admit that we are worthwhile in and of ourselves, that we deserve to care for ourselves in every way. Today a high priority is placed on personal fulfillment, on the quality of life. Once, achievement meant worldly success; today, it means thoughtful improvement of the self, involving such concepts as need, growth, and self-actualization.

When children are very small, their world centers on themselves. Everything is ME! I WANT! MINE! We laugh and indulge the toddlers, but soon we begin teaching them that there are other people who have rights, too, that they need to share and be part of the larger scene. It's sad that sometimes the sense of self gets lost in all this societal conditioning. There needs to be a balance between getting along in society and demanding self-fulfillment.

Contradictory Expectations

Children are taught that they can do anything they put their minds to. In our grandmothers' times, girls were limited, minorities were limited, disadvantaged people were limited. Today, while sexism, racism, and financial constraints still exist, there are opportunities despite the many obstacles. But such opportunities are usually very well defined, limited to jobs, careers, and work. How many children are told that they can take time off after college to travel, to "find themselves"? How many children are told that they don't have to pursue a career but can be housewives or househusbands? We think we have advanced so far, but how many young men would say that they don't want to work but would prefer to stay at home and rear their children? That may be their idea of personal fulfillment, but they don't dare voice it, for fear of being thought lazy, shiftless, and strange. On the one hand, we emphasize constantly that our children are part of the first generation to have so many choices, yet we tell them they are also the first generation that will not outdistance their parents in terms of educational level, life-style, or material possessions. Children often receive mixed messages of how they should go about *being* and *doing* in their world. We say "Be true to your feelings," in one breath, and "Do whatever it takes to succeed," in another. Such contradictory messages would confuse anyone, let alone an uncertain youngster.

Option Overload

Children today are bombarded by options and choices—in ideologies, careers, and life-styles. Among the many new possibilities:

- New fields of work
- Changing definitions of success
- Viable options in self-fulfillment
- A free conscience—perceptions of being free to choose
- Emphasis on making fewer sacrifices
- Expectations of enjoying the warmth of a relationship and/or family along with the freedom to choose this
- Defining new rules; redefining old ones
- Expectation of psychological satisfaction from a job
- Desire for personal autonomy
- Expectation of being treated with "dignity," "fairness," and "justice"
- Introspective thinking/problem solving
- New social ethic of commitment
- Emphasis on closer, deeper personal relationships
- Emphasis on balancing professional and private lives more equally

- Option of not marrying, having a family, and living a traditional life

That young people have more options doesn't necessarily mean they will make better choices. In fact, this can contribute to ambiguity and option overload—especially when teachers, parents, and other adult mentors spend less time guiding young people toward making wise choices.

Consider how the abundance of choices results in ambiguity, contributing to confusion and stress.

Dilemma: An abundance of choices about what to do with one's life but insufficient knowledge of how to make the right choice.

Stress: Because of the high value placed on personal freedom, each new commitment is considered a threat to that freedom and a challenge to the other options that might also be exercised, leading to confusion and quandary and, sometimes, total paralysis.

Dilemma: The preoccupation with physiological and psychological needs, which places a continual emphasis on the desires of the self. Emotions are sacred; not fulfilling one's needs is sacrilegious.

Stress: This psychological attitude affects precisely those crisis points in one's life when attention might more productively be turned outward toward the world and its vicissitudes.

Dilemma: The freedom for a woman to decide whether she will have children or concentrate wholeheartedly on her career without any distractions.

Stress: Women today have the option, for the first time in history, of remaining childless without much stigma attached to the decision by society at large. However, parents usually desire to have descendants, and not having a family is considered selfish by many.

Dilemma: The choice of a young man to spend more time with family and less with career. Men nowadays have the option of working fewer hours at less-demanding jobs and becoming more involved in the rearing and nurturing of their children.

Stress: Society still expects the male to be the primary bread-winner and sometimes indicates that "real men" don't give up a chance at making more money just to stay home with the children. The "wimp factor" comes into play.

Dilemma: The ever-increasing number of jobs and careers open to both women and men, including jobs that didn't exist just a generation or two ago (such as computer programmer, environmental activist, or doctor specializing in sports medicine).

Stress: Children are constantly asked what they want to be when they grow up; they are overwhelmed by the sheer number of opportunities available. They have heard of so many careers and jobs but know little about what those jobs entail. Yet they feel pressure to define themselves and their future by giving a response: "I want to be a biologist," "I want to be in food service."

What Are Your Child's Goals and Priorities? A Quiz

There's no disputing that our children have more options open to them than any other generation before them. For them to make the best choices, choices they can live with without excessive stress, it is vital that they be able to identify their priorities and preferences.

The following is an exercise I've written to help you and your children recognize what is important to them. Try the exercise on your own first. Answer the questions as you think your children would answer them. Avoid the temptation to answer as a "perfect child" would; be honest and respond as you believe your own children might. As you go through the questions, you will be identifying what you think your child's goals and priorities are. When you have finished the exercise, hand it to your child, without telling her you have already gone through it on her behalf. Have your child answer the questions as well, preferably without your input. Emphasize that there are no right or wrong answers and that she should be as honest as possible. Depending on the age of your child, you may have to reword some of these questions so that your child can understand them. For example, if your child is four years old, you might take the question "If you had a choice between being very rich so that you could buy anything, and being very popular so that everyone liked you, which would you prefer?" and reword it thus: "If you could chose only one, which would you rather have, a lot of money so that you could buy everything, or a lot of friends?"

Goals and Priorities Quiz

1. If you had a choice between being very rich so that you could buy anything, and being very popular so that everyone liked you, which would you prefer?

2. Which of the following would you most prefer to be: an internationally famous movie star, an unknown but brilliant research scientist, or a minister or social worker helping the poor? Why?

3. If you absolutely could not have both but had to choose only one, which would you rather have, an exciting career or a happy family life?

4. Which would you rather be, a well-known world-class athlete who frequently breaks under pressure or is injured and never wins the big competitions, or a small-time character actor who enjoys the work and makes decent money but never becomes well known?

5. If you were very rich, then suddenly lost all of your money, what would you do? Would you work hard to try to get rich again, or would you relax and do other things, like travel cheaply around the world or go sit on a beach and contemplate nature?

6. If you were considering marrying someone, and that person suddenly was in an accident and lost all ability to earn a living (but could still get around and do things), would you marry this person and support him all his life, or would you look for someone else?

7. If you had the choice of being a model in magazine and billboard ads for blue jeans, with your face and figure shown all over the country, or being a researcher who stays in a lab doing crucial work but is not known to the public at large, which would you choose?

8. If you were in love with someone who wanted to get married but never have children, would you marry that person or look for someone else who wanted children?

9. If you worked for twenty years and made enough money by the age of forty to retire and live a middle-class life for the rest of your life, would you do so? Or would you continue to work very hard and earn more money but not have as much leisure time as you would have if you retired?

10. If you were very ill and could choose between two types of treatment, one that is very painful but cures you quickly and lets you get back to a normal life in just a few months, and one that hardly hurts but wouldn't cure you for nearly a year, which would you choose?

Your children's responses will reveal a great deal about their values. After you talk with them about their preferences and why they chose as they did, discuss the choices or options you had and have, and why you did what you did. Ask your children what they would have done in your place . . . and try not to take their responses personally! If your son tells you that he would have worked less and spent more time with his friends, he is not criticizing you; rather, he may subconsciously be telling you that he feels stressed by doing so much work at school and misses the time he could spend just hanging out with his friends. If your daughter tells you that she would have had fewer children than you have, it doesn't mean she doesn't love her siblings. She may be telling you that she wants to spend more time taking care of herself and less time looking out for others.

If you are dissatisfied with your life, if you feel less than fulfilled, it is okay to discuss that with your children. Tell them why, and what you hope to do about it. Be wary of making the children feel that you are blaming them for not accomplishing all you wanted with your life. Help them understand that the happiest people are those who identify what will make them fulfilled and who then work toward that fulfillment.

The Spirituality Gap: Helping Your Child Find Meaning, Purpose, and Direction

The First Amendment provides for the religious preferences of all. But today, there remains almost a taboo against speaking of religion or spiritual beliefs and how they provide one with meaning, purpose, and direction. Yet, spirituality is often at the core of how we live our lives, establishing the guidelines to which we adhere in everyday interactions.

Examining the spiritual side of our lives and its role in our well-being should not be limited to a child's early Sunday School years, or discussed only among senior citizens or those who are terminally ill. A child who has a sense of his or her spirituality feels supported—he or she has a helpmate. When a child has faith, he has an inner strength that serves as a buffer in dealing with the traumatic times that occur in his life.

Moral and Spiritual Principles Are Life's Guideposts

Encourage your children to talk about their sense of spirituality. Spiritual principles guide children; they are a source of comfort and protection, and your children need to be made aware of this. The following is a list of topics you can discuss with your children to help them begin thinking about spirituality. Of course, you will want to adapt the questions to your children's ages and maturity levels.

- Do we have an obligation to do something special with our lives?

- How much responsibility do you feel for other people—family, friends, acquaintances, strangers? Do you think you have an obligation to help them, even if doing so could be uncomfortable for you?

- Are there things that you have no control over? Why do you think those things happen?

- Why do bad things happen, even to people who are very good or are trying their best? Why do bad people who do terrible things sometimes succeed more than good people?

- How do you feel after doing something nice for someone? Why do you feel that way?

- Do you think there is a spirit that moves us to be kind and do good deeds?

- When are you most comfortable with yourself? When do you like yourself the most? When do you dislike yourself the most?

- Why do you think there are rules for behavior? Do you think it's wrong to do something bad if no one will catch you, or if it seems no one will be hurt by it?

- When you say your prayers, who do you think is listening? Have your prayers been answered? Do you think there are right and wrong things to pray for? What are they?

- If you have done something bad, how can you make up for it? What can you do to feel better about yourself?

- What kinds of religions have you heard about, from your teachers or from your friends? Do you see any points in common among these religions? Why do you suppose so many different religions have developed over the years?

- Do you think your opinions about God, about good and evil, will change as you get older? Is that okay?

Parents Are Spiritual Role Models

Let your children see the role that spirituality plays in your own life. Don't be afraid to discuss with them how you feel about the larger issues. Too often we sell children short, thinking they won't be able to understand the "big" concepts, such as our mission, our calling, our purpose in life. Yet this can be very comforting to children. Like adults, children thirst to know about themselves and their relationship to something bigger, all-knowing, all-powerful. Children too want to believe that there is some reason for their existence. When a child sees the positive role that spirituality plays in your life, that it will succor you throughout your life, he will make it an important part of his own life.

This chapter has focused on the outer world your children live in and the challenges they encounter there. The next chapter examines the inner world of your child and explores ways to help your child manage the more immediate challenges of growing and developing.

PART II

Understanding the Nature of Stress

Chapter 3

WHAT IS STRESS?

B art Simpson or Beavis and Butt-head have been their role models. They have grown up seeing pictures of their peers on milk cartons. They are familiar with talk about AIDS. One of their parents likely has lost a job or has had to switch careers to earn a living. One in five of them has been born to an unmarried mother. Many have spent at least part of their lives in homes with only one parent. Two out of three have mothers who work outside the home. Fast food and fast service are what they expect. They want the American Dream—a nice house, a nice car, a good job, vacations in great places, and a loving family.

These are today's children. Compare the stressors they encounter to those we faced when we were their age and you can see how important it is that we help them cope with what awaits them.

Why Children Are Not Immune to Stress

It's clear that chronic stress prolonged beyond reasonable bounds can precipitate major health breakdowns. Young people may be even more vulnerable because so much of their existence involves continual change, clarification of values, and forced choices. Unexpected or unfamiliar situations requiring as-yet-unlearned coping skills produce a great deal of stress for children. Added to this is the difficulty that children may be either unable to articulate their problems or afraid to say what's troubling them. It's a myth that children are somehow more resilient; children are as vulnerable to stress as adults are. There are as many events in the lives of children that cause them stress as there are in our own adult lives.

How traumatic is it to lose a pet, have a friend move away, be under constant scrutiny, experience a teacher's ridicule, be rejected by your peer group, or deal with the separation or divorce of your parents? How much emotional anxiety is involved? How does stress impair a young person's ability to function in healthy and appropriate ways? What is stressful to children?

No One Consulted Danny

Eleven-year-old Danny began having severe headaches. At first his parents thought the headaches might mean that he needed glasses. An eye exam ruled that out. Next came extensive tests for allergies, and then other medical tests. When no physical causes for the headaches could be found, his parents sought the help of a child psychologist. As Danny began to open up about what was bothering him, his parents learned that his headaches stemmed from the emotional pain he was feeling about his best friend's moving some 1,300 miles away.

Andy had been Danny's "best bud." The two boys were always doing things together: They frequently helped each other with homework, rode bikes or played catch after school, were on the same soccer and baseball teams. They sat with each other on the bus every day; they shared balls, bats, and baseball gloves. They were like brothers.

Andy's mother, an account representative for a computer firm, was growing weary of single-parenting and longed to return to the Midwest, where her parents and brothers and sisters lived. She submitted her request for a transfer hoping that it would come through within a year. When a position opened only two months later, she faced a decision: How would she maintain her rigorous work schedule, find suitable housing for herself and her son in another city, schedule the move, and make the transition as smooth as possible for her son? Because her schedule took her away from home so often, and because she did not want her son to feel unsupported as he faced the enormity of the changes that lay ahead, she decided to get things in order and tell him as the time for moving approached. She told her son of the move only one week prior to the moving van's showing up! Andy scarcely had time to comprehend what was happening.

No one had prepared either boy for the trauma he was about to experience. With little time to share the reality of being separated, both boys were devastated. For Danny, losing his best friend seemed like an insurmountable loss. How he pined for Andy.

As it turned out, Danny's physical illness was a symptom of his mourning his friend. He sorely needed help to come to terms with his loss, and guidance in finding ways to preserve the cherished friendship. Fortunately, Danny's parents listened to his fears about losing his friend and allowed him to grieve without making their son feel inadequate. They explained to him that separation didn't necessarily mean the end of friendship, and they helped him create solutions to his dilemma. They helped him see that he could write letters, phone (with permission), and even arrange summer or holiday get-togethers with his friend. Through his parents' genuine interest in helping Danny cope with the loss of his friend, he was able to feel more powerful in preserving the friendship and better able to accept that the stress he was feeling was a natural part of his loss. Though he still misses his friend, his physical symptoms have subsided.

Cartoons Are Not for Sissies

Some years ago I took my daughter, then eight, to the doctor for a blood test. My daughter cried, pleaded with me not to have the test done, and kicked the walls on the way to the lab. At the lab door, she screamed and refused to enter. She then fainted. After she recovered and we had left the office, I sat with her on the lawn outside the medical complex. Nearly thirty minutes later I learned the source of her fear. It seems that she had seen cartoons in which shots were given maliciously, with very long needles. My daughter proceeded to describe a foot-long needle, which she imagined would start at the base of her wrist and extend to her elbow. Under no circumstance was she about to be victim to that!

After debunking the myth, describing the actual procedure,

and agreeing that she first be allowed to watch blood being drawn, I got her cooperation. She was then able to go through with the relatively painless (though scary) procedure in a relaxed manner. I had to trust that my daughter's fears were real and painful, and she had to trust that my control over ensuing matters would take into account her fear and sensitivity to pain.

Children Burn Out, Too

No one could understand Jena's running away from home. At sixteen, she was a cheerleader and a good student, and she was close to her mother and brother. With the best of intentions, Jena's mother wanted her to have all the advantages and so arranged for her to have clarinet lessons, foreign-language classes, ballet lessons, tennis instruction, and a pet to care for. To Jena's mother, it seemed like a wholesome and balanced agenda of activities. As Jena sees it, it was fun at first. "It was also pretty grueling. I just ran by the schedule. But one day I forgot my 'to do' list at home, and I couldn't even function! After two semesters of this schedule, the days blurred into weeks, the weeks into months. I don't even remember the past four months. I just got so tired. Soon it became more work than fun. I felt I just couldn't go on. I no longer wanted to be a National Merit Scholar finalist, first-chair clarinet, or an editor of the school paper."

To cope, Jena tried remedies suggested by her friends—from diet pills to No-Doz—to tackle her agenda. "I even found myself stealing diet pills from the grocery store when my allowance wouldn't cover them," said Jena, but after a while, even those didn't work. "I would be really wound up for the first few hours and then experience this incredible tiredness by noon. I resigned from student government, began skipping a class here and there, and started to copy homework assignments from friends. I felt so down on myself, like I had really let everyone down, especially my parents."

At that point, Jena went to a friend's house and refused to go home to her parents. When her mother went to see her, Jena would not agree to come back, threatening to "disappear" if her mother "forced her" to return. She was gone for eleven days and did not attend school during that time.

Jena is back home now. With the help and support of her mother and the family physician, along with family counseling, she is regaining her health and is slowly rebuilding her confidence to cope with daily life. Jena's case may seem overly exaggerated, almost melodramatic, but it is not uncommon.

Stress is a familiar word these days. But what is it, really? How does it impair our children's lives? What are the major pressures, fears, and strains that keep our children from learning, achieving, and excelling, from developing close friendships with other children, and from establishing better relationships with their parents? What can we do to lessen the toll? Knowing exactly what stress is and how it translates into human suffering can be an important first step.

What Is Stress?

Stress is the name we give to the reaction of the body when it mobilizes its defenses against demands made upon it. It is the body's physical, emotional, and chemical reaction to circumstances that cause confusion, irritation, or excitement. The adrenal glands are the body's prime reactors to stress, which can be induced by a negative *or* a positive stimulus.

You probably remember hearing about the "fight or flight" syndrome—the body's natural response to a threat in order to protect itself. In stress situations, the body has an instinctive chemical response pattern designed to supply energy. The activity of certain glands is triggered by a threat, called a *stressor*, in the body's environment. Typical stressors are strong emotions, physical illness, and drugs. The body reacts to each demand made upon it in a different and appropriate manner. For example, when you are too cold, you shiver to produce heat; when you are too warm, you perspire to reduce body temperature.

When exposed to stressors—such as a physical threat or an emotional crisis—the body experiences a need to restore itself to a normal state. Conscious and unconscious efforts to adapt to situations or pressures trigger a chain of biological events. These physiological changes take place in the body processes and in the electrochemical system. The hormone adrenaline, for example, speeds up the pulse rate and blood pressure, simultaneously raising the level of blood sugar. The hormone insulin, on the other hand, decreases the level of blood sugar. When the body needs to adjust to a stressor in order to maintain a normal balance, or stasis, it undergoes what is called "general adaptation syndrome." This nonspecific demand for response activity is the essence of stress (see Illustration #1).

The Biology of Stress

Stress, then, is a biological occurrence, a response to a demand by the body for readjustment. The body experiences stress in situations that are both positive, such as having friends over for a dinner party, and negative, such as making a court appearance.

Illustration #1
General Adaptation Syndrome

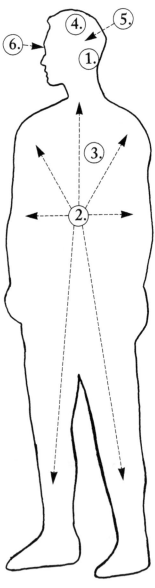

1.

A small portion of the brain called the hypothalmus has triggered the pituitary gland, located near the base of the brain. Its hormone, ACTH, is released into the bloodstream.

2.

ACTH goes directly to the adrenal glands, which then step up their output of adrenaline into the bloodstream, along with related hormones called corticoids. These hormones bring your body up to its aroused state. Within the first eight seconds, the bloodstream has carried these stress organizers into every cell in the body. At the same time, commands are traveling through the nerve communication system to alert heart, lungs, and muscles for action. The muscles have been more richly supplied with blood as the tiny vessels constrict and the blood pressure increases. Blood has been diverted away from the extremities. The liver, too, is working harder to convert its stored glycogen into glucose, which the brain and muscles will need in greater supply.

3.

Meanwhile, breathing becomes rapid, increasing the amount of oxygen in the blood, which enables the muscles and the brain to burn that glucose more efficiently. The heart is pumping, sending an abundant supply of blood to the priority portions of the body. Skeletal muscles brace.

4.

The brain is busy with preparations for physical action—one reason why it becomes difficult to think effectively on abstract levels during this panic state.

5.

Hearing may become more acute.

6.

The pupils of the eyes dilate, making vision more acute.

Stressors may be physical or emotional. Regardless of the source or type of stressor, the body's reaction to stress develops in three distinct stages. These are (1) the alarm reaction, (2) resistance/ adaptation, and (3) exhaustion/burnout. Let's examine each phase more closely.

PHASE I: THE ALARM REACTION

The alarm reaction phase notifies the body to act. In this phase, the body begins to gear up and prepares to take action. In your own experience, you can probably recall many of the alarm re- action responses initiated by the autonomic nervous system.

- **Nervous stomach.** Our stomachs become queasy and fluttery when digestion slows so that blood may be directed where it is needed more, such as the muscles and the brain, in preparation for fight or flight.

- **Rapid breathing.** Breathing accelerates in order to supply more oxygen to the muscles, so they can be "jump started" as needed.

- **Pounding heart.** The heart speeds up and blood pressure soars, forcing blood to parts of the body that need to take action.

- **Perspiration.** Perspiration increases to cool the body, allowing it to burn more energy.

- **"Second wind."** Sugars and fats pour into the bloodstream to provide fuel for quick energy, increasing alertness, strength, and endurance.

Illustration #2
The Two Stress Cycles: Distress and Wellness

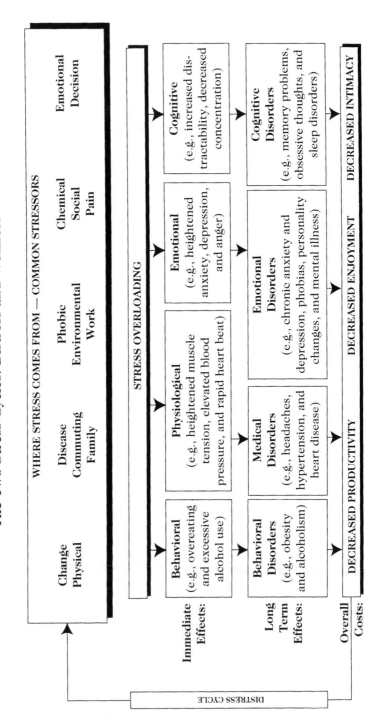

The Two Stress Cycles: Distress and Wellness

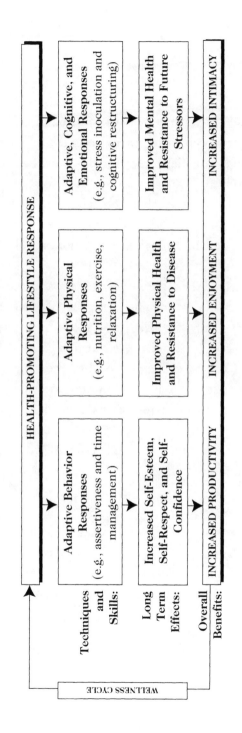

HEALTH-PROMOTING LIFESTYLE RESPONSE

Techniques and Skills:

| Adaptive Behavior Responses (e.g., assertiveness and time management) | Adaptive Physical Responses (e.g., nutrition, exercise, relaxation) | Adaptive, Cognitive, and Emotional Responses (e.g., stress inoculation and cognitive restructuring) |

Long Term Effects:

| Increased Self-Esteem, Self-Respect, and Self-Confidence | Improved Physical Health and Resistance to Disease | Improved Mental Health and Resistance to Future Stressors |

Overall Benefits:

| INCREASED PRODUCTIVITY | INCREASED ENJOYMENT | INCREASED INTIMACY |

WELLNESS CYCLE

PHASE II: RESISTANCE/ADAPTATION

The body always seeks to be balanced, to be in stasis. Because during Phase I biochemical changes have occurred to upset that balance, the body attempts to regain the balance in Phase II. This resistance stage essentially reverses the processes of the alarm stage. The body attempts to return to calm and tranquility by lowering body temperature, blood pressure, heart rate, and respiration. If this phase is successful, the physical signs of stress disappear: Muscles relax, breathing returns to normal. The body is resisting the source of the stress.

The problem occurs when the stress persists and the body continues to react to it with ongoing accelerated heartbeat and muscle tensing. Eventually, the adaptation mechanisms are depleted, causing the body to enter the exhaustion stage. Certain bodily reactions become fixed. A great deal of energy and vital resources are required in this stage, and in the process, essential minerals and vitamins necessary for healthy functioning are depleted. Notice, in Illustration #2, how short-term, negative coping can lead to long-term problems while effective intervention can lead to positive outcomes.

PHASE III: EXHAUSTION/BURNOUT

When the body has used up all of its adaptation energy and isn't able to cope anymore, exhaustion or burnout results. The body's ability to resist stress is gone. Body damage occurs from the constant physical wear and tear. So-called diseases of adaptation may occur. Have you ever noticed, for example, how quickly you catch a cold or the flu when your resistance is low, and how long the cold seems to linger? Your body no longer can fight off the stressors.

Stress becomes pathological when your body reacts long after the normal threat has passed. For example, elevated blood pressure under stress is a normal reaction, but when it persists, it becomes hypertension. A pounding heart may be diagnosed as tachycardia. A blood shift away from the stomach, if prolonged, may lead to a lack of appetite.

Psychosomatic Disease

Psychosomatic refers to mental and bodily symptoms stemming from mental conflict. The basis is that the mind plays an important role in protecting the body from disease; conversely, it can also weaken the body and make it more susceptible to illness. Psychosomatic conditions fall into two categories: psychogenic and somatogentic. Both affect the function and structure of the body.

Psychogenic disorders are physical diseases caused by emotional stress (fear, anxiety, grief). Actual structural and functional organ damage may occur, yet none of the usual underlying physical causes of organic disease are present. Conditions that fall into this category include bronchial asthma, skin reactions, backaches, peptic ulcers, and migraine headaches. These disorders may manifest themselves when a person is not coping adequately with life. Emotional turmoil, if long-term, can lead to more severe conditions.

Somatogenic disorders are organic diseases and infections brought on by emotional disturbances. When a person is under more stress than he or she is able to handle, latent infection can be converted into organic diseases. Normally, a healthy body fights off invading organisms through its natural defense mechanisms.

When stress impedes this defensive role, the immune system is hampered and the result is a breakdown in physical health. The onset or removal of intense or prolonged stress may accelerate or slow the rate at which disease spreads through the body; stress may be linked, for example, to spontaneous remission or relapse of diseases such as multiple sclerosis and cancer.

One Person's Stress May Not Be Yours

Stress is an individual matter. To a businessperson, stress may be the tension he or she experiences from the frustration of having too many things to do and not enough time to do them. An educator may see it as exhaustion from teaching many students, all at different ability levels. An air traffic controller may view stress as an overload, detrimental to concentration, while an athlete may perceive stress as a state of mind necessary for good performance. A young person may see it as related to specific situations—taking a quiz, dealing with a friend who doesn't save him a seat on the bus, being upset with a parent. What is stressful to one person may not be to another. How each responds is somewhat dependent on the power he assigns to the stressor, that is, how important he feels it is. How violently or calmly we respond to a stressor is generally a learned response, and it is under our own control. Each of us interprets and assigns different meanings (power) to the stressors in our lives.

Why some individuals become ill and others thrive under the same stressful conditions is determined by the person's interpretation of the stressor. While one person is slightly discomfited by a situation, experiencing a momentary headache and nervousness, another person is severely incapacitated by it, suffering emotional despair and psychosomatic illness.

Tawny and Lila

Consider how two schoolgirls respond to losing their backpacks. Tawny gets to school, sees her backpack is missing, looks in her locker, then realizes she must have left it in her mother's car that morning. She is annoyed with herself for being careless, concerned that she will inconvenience her mother, and slightly worried that when she calls her mom to bring the pack she'll have to listen to a lecture on being more responsible. She begrudges the time she'll have to wait for the backpack to be brought to her. As soon as Tawny's mother delivers the backpack, the stress is put behind her; the whole situation has caused no more than minor irritation.

Lila has a different response. When she sees her backpack is missing, she makes a frantic search, looking not only in her locker but in her friends' lockers, in the cafeteria and library, all over the school. She rushes around for a half hour, becoming more and more frazzled. She is unable to concentrate, gets knots in her stomach, is close to tears. When she finally realizes that maybe she left the pack in her mother's car, she panics, adding more stress by thinking that perhaps her mother will be furious with her for having to take the time to come back to school to drop it off. Lila dithers, not knowing whether to call her mom or go through the day without her pack, which she knows she needs. Her ability to think clearly, to solve what should be a minor problem, has vanished. Lila is very stressed out; her whole day is shot.

Each girl had the same cause for stress, but each reacted differently. Tawny took steps quickly to solve the problem, while Lila's stress debilitated her.

Managing stress is about learning how to manage our individual response to stressful situations. By understanding stress and how we respond to it, by knowing what specific strategies or coping behaviors can be used to reduce stress, we can protect our bodies against the ravages of stress. By learning to moderate its negative effects, we can learn to draw vitality from it as well.

The Mind/Body Connection

Stress provokes a number of chemical changes in the body that have profound effects on physical and mental health alike. Because stress triggers chemical changes in the brain and alters the body's chemical balance, it is thought to be a causative factor in a number of health breakdowns and has been associated with the development of many diseases. According to a 1983 article in *Time*, stress is now known to be a "major contributor to coronary heart disease, cancer, lung ailments, accidental injuries, cirrhosis of the liver, and suicide—six of the leading causes of death in the U.S. . . . . Stress also plays a role in aggravating such diverse conditions as multiple sclerosis, diabetes, and even psychiatric disorders."

Perhaps the most significant new discovery about stress is its deleterious effect on the immune system. Researchers have discovered that the body's production of its own cancer-fighting cells, including natural killer cells, T-lymphocytes, and macrophages, is inhibited by chronic stress. AIDS patients are taught to do everything possible to limit their stress in order to build up their T-cell counts. Stress lowers the T-cell count, leaving

AIDS patients more vulnerable to opportunistic infections, including pneumonia and other respiratory diseases.

Many experts believe that the mind and body influence each other and work in harmony in sickness and in health. This connection is illustrated by the formerly life-threatening condition called marasmus, associated with infants in hospitals who lost vitality and died for no apparent reason, despite adequate diets and sterile conditions. The researchers who examined the problem found that the babies who didn't die were those who were held and cuddled more often by the nurses. When the nurses were ordered to "mother" all of the babies, to hold and stroke them a certain amount of time each day, marasmus was eliminated. It seems that infants cannot grow or thrive unless they experience physical and emotional closeness with another human being.

The need for connection never goes away. It goes on throughout life. In its absence, symptoms develop—from the angry acting-out of the adolescent to depression, addiction, and illness. In her work with troubled teens, family therapist Lori Gordon discovered that troubled and disturbed adolescents often lacked the nurturing environment they regarded as crucial for healthy growth. Because the teenagers' problems were rooted in their troubled relationships with their parents, their recovery was *dependent* upon receiving emotional support and affection from their parents. Dr. Gordon found that when parents were taught about the importance of demonstrating affection toward their teens and followed through by becoming more supportive, only then could teens begin the process of losing their anger and move on to become active and productive in worthwhile causes.

The idea that psychological forces play an active role in the development of some emotional illnesses and diseases, and that other psychological forces can be mobilized to defeat them or delay their course, is gaining widespread attention. Dr. Ken Pelletier, author of the widely acclaimed *Mind as Healer, Mind as Slayer*, believes that all disorders are psychosomatic in the sense that both mind and body are involved in their origin. "Any disorder is created out of a complex interaction of social factors, physical and psychological stress, the personality of the person subjected to these influences, and the inability of the person to adapt adequately to pressures." Dr. Pelletier also believes that a medical symptom may be a useful signal of the need for change in other parts of the person's life.

Lawrence LeShan, author of *You Can Fight for Your Life*, and a number of other researchers believe that while the mechanism whereby stressful events produce illness is presumably physiological, mental hardiness may decrease the likelihood of breakdown into illness. For example, one individual may develop stress-related symptoms (such as ulcers, colitis, migraine headaches, hypertension, heart disease) during stressful seasons in his or her work, while a colleague holding the same or a similarly demanding job experiences no such setbacks and, in fact, seems to thrive on stress. That one person does well under stress while another develops stress-related illness and disease supports the contention that the degree to which individuals experience stress depends to a large extent on how they appraise the stressful situation.

Life-Change Stress
Some experts believe that critical events or changes in our lives can trigger stress in even the most hardy of us and can even cause physical, mental, and emotional illnesses. At Johns

Hopkins University, Dr. Caroline Bedell Thomas has correlated psychological factors with the long-term health records of 1,337 medical students who graduated between 1948 and 1964. Two of the strongest predictors of cancer, mental illness, and suicide were "lack of closeness to parents" and "a negative attitude toward one's family." Other studies show similar results. Dr. Thomas H. Holmes, a psychiatrist at the University of Washington School of Medicine, and his colleagues constructed a scale of stress values measured in "life change units" (LCU) to test this theory. Stress scores are attached to specific life events over a one-year period. A score of 150 or less indicates a 35 percent chance a person will get sick or have an accident within the next two years; a score of 150–300 means the chance of an accident or illness within the next two years is 51 percent; a score over 300 means the chance is 80 percent. (The complete Holmes-Rahe Scale can be found in the back of this book.)

Stress may not be caused so much by major life-change events themselves as by the ripples and repercussions stemming from those events. A single traumatic event, such as the loss of a job or a divorce, can cause other changes that are the more potent stressors. For example, divorce is often accompanied by isolation, a reduction in income, and single parenthood. Joblessness can have a similar ripple effect—it may not be the loss of a job itself that is the stressor but rather the domestic and psychological changes it imposes.

Factors in Coping Well with Stress

Some individuals manage well under stress and pressure, even flourish on it. How do they do it? It seems that far more important than the trials and tribulations in one's life is how one deals with them—in other words, what kind of *coping behaviors* one uses. Investigation into the coping behaviors of Vietnam prisoners of war, for example, reveals that communication with fellow captives, sometimes involving complex tapping codes, and maintaining a sense of control over their environment were vital factors in their survival. Former POW Jim Stockdale said that even while he was being beaten by his captors, he could hear other prisoners tapping out the supportive message "God bless you, Jim Stockdale."

Psychologists believe that a number of personal factors are helpful in coping. Among them:

- high self-esteem
- the sense of being in control of one's life
- having a network of friends or family to provide support
- personality factors such as flexibility and hopefulness
- the ability to express feelings and emotions openly
- being honest
- having a sense of humor
- being able to adjust to problems
- having satisfying work
- having a confidential relationship with someone trustworthy
- being able to get along well with others
- being a good listener

High-stress/low-illness individuals reduce the intensity of stressors by taking an active role in their work and family lives. Social supports such as family, friends, and colleagues serve as buffers against stress. Such individuals view their activities as interesting, important, and as having an impact on their surroundings. These attitudes give them a feeling of being in control of their lives, another element of psychological hardiness. Those who thrive on challenge make a point of seeing the cup half full as opposed to half empty; they see life as a journey to be lived, not a problem to be solved. They are more likely to say, "When you get lemons, make lemonade," or "If your ship hasn't come in, swim out to it."

In contrast, for people who rate low in psychological hardiness, stress has debilitating effects since the stressor remains in their minds unassimilated and unaltered, an issue of endless rumination and subconscious preoccupation. They may use avoidance techniques to cope, but excessive use or abuse of alcohol and drugs, use of tranquilizers, excess sleeping, or escape through endless hours of television viewing will alleviate stress for only a short while.

The Buffer of Self-Esteem

Self-esteem is self-regard; it's how much a person values himself. There is a logical connection between self-esteem and how well individuals handle stress. Adults and children who possess a positive sense of self-worth are more likely to put stress into perspective and avoid assigning too much importance to the stressor. Because they see themselves as capable and competent people, able to manage the ups and downs of life, they begin an effort to cope. They do what is necessary to make the stressor go away. On the other hand, those with low self-esteem tend to cope poorly with stress either because they don't have faith that they can and will prevail, or because their low sense of self-worth rarely affords the courage to risk doing the things that make the stress go away. Instead, they fall prey to being a bystander or a victim of stress.

Parents can help their children develop healthy and positive self-esteem, which can serve as a buffer for stress, by strengthening six vital areas:

Six Ingredients of Self-Esteem

1. Physical safety. Children must feel that they are safe in their homes, neighborhoods, schools. They must learn to care about their bodies and avoid doing things to jeopardize them, such as taking drugs, drinking alcohol, or falling prey to bulimia or obesity.

2. Emotional security. When parents refrain from ridiculing or humiliating their children, when children have the comfort of knowing they can take risks and fail without their parents making them feel bad about the failure, they attempt new things and learn from their mistakes. They feel they are worthy of respect, and they treat others the same way.

3. Identity. Children must learn about themselves and their individuality. They need to become friends with the face in the mirror.

4. Belonging. Children need to feel loved by family and friends. Children who feel accepted, liked, and respected know they have a support system that can help them deal with the knocks that life sometimes gives them. They are comfortable being who they are and don't have to pretend to be something or someone they are not.

5. Competence. When a parent helps her children become competent at something, she makes them feel capable not only in that area but in other facets of their lives as well. Feeling capable gives children the motivation to achieve. They believe they can cope with challenges, overcome problems, deal with stress. They are willing to try new things and to persevere rather than give up when the going gets rough.

6. Meaning and purpose. Children need to set and work toward goals that are important to them. They need to have a value system they understand and can relate to. Life has direction, is fun and worthwhile, when meaning and purpose are clear. Children without meaning and purpose conclude that they are without value.

When children possess healthy self-esteem, they are more capable of dealing with the stress and strains of life without falling apart. Learn about self-esteem and how you as a parent can develop and nurture it in your children. Excellent resources for developing self-esteem are listed in the Suggested Readings section in the back of this book.

You can't always protect your children completely from stress, of course, nor should you. No life is going to be without stress, certainly not a child's life, in which each day offers new learning experiences. Trial and error confront children daily, from their school studies to learning how to accept, appreciate, and deal with the diversity of others. Children are about doing, experimenting, taking action. Exploring the world about them, they will undoubtedly get into a few scrapes. Children must become capable of dealing with the stress, strains, and pressures that are sure to be a part of their lives. Be sure that you help your child learn coping skills in managing stress; do not leave your child to his or her own devices in learning these skills. If you do that, you run the risk that your child will sucumb to stress or learn to cope in ways that are not appropriate. Dropping out of school, for example, is a not an appropriate coping response in the face of a lack of good study habits or a need for assertive skills in dealing with peers. You can help your child learn good stress management skills. (Part V of this book is designed to help your children develop specific stress management skills.)

The connection between stress and illness has been established. While some events cause significantly more stress than others, even small stressors can take their toll. This is especially true for children, who often lack the ability to change their circumstances. While adults can switch jobs, for instance, and choose the adults with whom they will live or socialize, children are powerless to switch schools, parents, or schoolmates. The key is to manage one's response to stress. Children need to be taught successful ways of coping with day-to-day stresses, and to learn how to meet the challenges of excessive stress in times of crises. When children are prepared, they feel empowered and develop confidence in themselves and their abilities to handle stress with success.

Chapter 4

HOW DO CHILDREN
EXPERIENCE STRESS?

Stress-Related Illness in Children

Stress-related chronic diseases and illnesses among children in America, the most affluent country in the world, are at an extraordinary high just when we might assume that they would be diminishing. Even with advances in medical science and the steady proliferation of programs designed to heighten our awareness of and commitment to the well-being of children, we find the incidence of stress in children is rising sharply.

The U.S. Government Health Agency, the National Center for Vital and Health Statistics, and other health agencies all report that chronic diseases and illnesses among American youngsters are on the rise. A national survey reported by *Time* magazine in 1988 found that two-thirds of teachers regarded "poor health" among children created learning problems.

As we had hoped, the incidence of communicable diseases of early childhood has fallen off dramatically since 1945, and infectious diseases, formerly major health hazards, are at an all-time low. This is due in part to new therapeutic procedures, improved sanitation, and advances in immunology. Data from the Department of Health, Education, and Welfare indicate a 144 percent decrease in the death rate for children from influenza and pneumonia in the past forty-five years.

Even with the decline in the incidence of acute disease, more youngsters are susceptible to a greater number of diseases and illnesses. The rate of heart disease among American children is now the highest in the world, with asthma ranking as the second most prevalent chronic condition among children. There are now numerous cases of babies born with malignancies, and cardiovascular diseases and birth defects have almost tripled in their rate of occurrence in the past twenty-five years. Chronic disease and illness among American youngsters increases with age: ten- to sixteen-year-olds are most frequently affected. In 1967, nearly 25 percent of youngsters under the age of sixteen suffered from one or more chronic diseases or illnesses, an increase of nearly 6 percent over the previous decade. According to the National Health Survey's study, one youngster out of every ten is reported to have a serious allergy, and asthma is the primary cause of school absences for young children.

Of particular significance in regard to the increased rate of chronic disease and illness among the young is the fact that there has been an increase in the number of youngsters experiencing *stress-related* illness and disease. The number of ulcers diagnosed among fifteen- to twenty-four-year-olds has risen sharply and is continuing to rise.

Children Are Second-Class Citizens— Beginning before Birth

We often speak of children as our future, but we act as if the future can take care of itself. As Marian Wright Edelman, founder of the Children's Defense Network, says, "The inattention to children by our society poses a greater threat to our safety, harmony, and productivity than any external enemy."

Expenditures on prenatal care is money well spent. Every dollar spent on care for pregnant women can save more than three dollars in medical bills during the child's first year, and another ten dollars within the next five years. Most investors would leap at the chance to earn that type of return on their money. Yet prenatal care in the United States is sorely lacking, as our infant mortality rates demonstrate. In America, there are 9.7 deaths per 1,000 births, a rate worse than 17 other developed countries. In the District of Columbia, there are 23 infant deaths per 1,000 births, a rate worse than that of Jamaica or Costa Rica. A 1990 article in *Time* magazine reported that each year more than a quarter-million babies are born seriously underweight, giving them a two to three times greater chance of being blind, deaf, or mentally retarded at birth. Infants like these may be kept in intensive care units, at a cost of $3,000 per child per day. Basic medical monitoring of a pregnant woman can cost as little as $500 for the whole term of the pregnancy.

There are, of course, programs in place to help improve child care. In 1974, Congress approved the Special Supplemental

Food Program for Women, Infants, and Children (known as WIC). WIC gives women vouchers to buy the foods that children need, including milk, formula, and juices. At only $30 a month for the vouchers, the program costs less than a dinner for two at a nice restaurant. Yet the government has put so little money into the program that less than 60 percent of the women and infants who qualify for the program are accepted.

The same lack of spending applies to medicine. In 1993, 12 percent of the gross national product, approximately 660 billion dollars, will go toward medical services, but only a small part of that will be spent on what has been shown to be one of the best services for children, preventive inoculations. In California alone, only half of all two-year-olds are fully immunized. The papers often report cases of young children dying needlessly from diseases, such as measles, for which immunizations are available. While the elderly have plans such as Medicare, there is no one set plan providing equivalent care for children. The health programs for youth are reviewed annually, and thus are subject to recessions and to budget-cutting programs. The major burden of health care for children is placed on their parents, many of whom are unable to pay for it.

In short, many children begin their lives already at a disadvantage. They may have birth defects, or they may be subject to childhood diseases or medical problems that lead to learning difficulties and other stresses later.

The lack of funding goes beyond medical programs, affecting child care and education as well. In Los Angeles County, there are no mandatory training programs for foster parents, who earn about 80 cents an hour caring for children (often those with special physical or emotional needs). Across the country, there are stories of unlicensed child care facilities that hire workers who were unable to obtain jobs anywhere else. The prevalent thinking seems to be, "I may not have a skill, but *anyone* can watch a bunch of kids." Because there is no state or national child care policy, parents are left to choose child care facilities on their own. Many parents have neither the expertise nor the time to screen the facilities and staff. Worse, they may not have the luxury of being able to afford the child care facility they know is the best. Children therefore are left at child care centers that are understaffed and overcrowded, resulting in stress to the children. The children are "cared for" in some cases by people who resent their jobs or who are doing it simply to get a paycheck. Children are likely to fall prey to these feelings of resentment, indifference, and rejection.

According to a 1993 article in *U.S. News & World Report*, there are more than 23 million American children under the age of six, and an estimated 9 million need full-time care, yet only about 5 million licensed-day-care slots are available. It is estimated that 10 million children need care before or after school—with slots for just 1.5 million to 3 million. Parents, teachers, psychiatrists, and children say this is "America's biggest secret: that millions of children are left in charge of other children because there is no one else."

Conditions do not improve as a child grows older. Many school systems are bankrupt, or nearly so, and have either cut teachers' salaries (which were not high to begin with) or cut the size of the faculty, resulting in a higher student-to-teacher ratio. Overcrowded schools in aging facilities with few books and overworked teachers cannot help but add to a child's stress (both subconscious and conscious). Subconsciously, children feel the pressure put on them when they are jostled in the hall or given scant attention in the classroom. All of this school stress eventually contributes to an increase in spending for juvenile halls and for the rehabilitation of young criminals.

There are many youngsters who commit crimes, and many more who appear ready to enter into a serious criminal life. We read newspaper stories of eight-year-olds who act as lookouts for drug pushers and fifteen-year-olds who sell the drugs and do so fearlessly because, should they be caught, they can't be tried as adults. When these children are arrested, they are put through the court system and usually sent to juvenile "rehabilitation" centers. While some such centers provide good treatment, too many others are merely holding tanks in which children are kept until their release date.

Recognizing Stress in Children: Signs and Symptoms

Sometimes we parents offer our children reassurance for their problems with such bromides as "Oh, don't worry; things will work out," or "Everything is bound to turn out okay; don't let it get to you." We seek to momentarily soothe the child without fully understanding the anxieties underlying the pain he or she is feeling. When we aren't sensitive to the stress our children are experiencing, we forfeit the chance to help them learn healthy ways to handle such feelings as loss, powerlessness, fear, anger, and hurt.

Even the most sensitive parent with his or her antennae fully extended might miss some of the more subdued stress reactions. For example, a usually rambunctious child might become quiet for a day or two. Instead of getting to the heart of what is causing the withdrawal, the parent may welcome a time of reprieve. The same is true when a child begins to exhaust his energy earlier than usual for more than a day at a time. The need for extra sleep might be an indicator of stress, but to the parent, it's just serendipity.

Some stress reactions are not so quiescent; they may include heart palpitations, insomnia, headaches, muscle tension, even ulcers. Following is a general list of emotional signs and physical symptoms of stress.

EMOTIONAL SIGNS OF STRESS

- a pervasive nervousness, comments of annoyance and irritation
- complaints of feeling like a victim, of being trapped with no way out
- frequent outbursts of uncontrollable temper
- apparent "blue" or lonely feelings
- apathy about appearance
- lack of interest in things once enjoyed, dropping out of previously enjoyed clubs, friendships, or activities
- changes in school performance
- constant fearfulness
- vacillating peaks and valleys of self-esteem
- remarks about feeling inferior
- difficulty making decisions

- over- or underexercising (more or less activity than usual)
- avoidance of others or frequent expressions of desire to be alone
- comments indicating hopelessness about the future

PHYSICAL SYMPTOMS OF STRESS
- tightening of muscles
- recurring headaches
- pains in the heart or chest
- pains in the lower back or neck or shoulders
- pounding or racing heart
- nausea or upset stomach
- loss of concentration
- dramatic change in food craving or general disinterest in food
- sleep difficulties (over- or undersleeping)
- weakness in parts of the body
- continual low energy or periods of high energy followed by depression

Charting Your Child's Stress

Did you catch yourself becoming alarmed when you read the list of stress-related signs and symptoms because you think your child may have a good many of them? Everyone has them at one time or another. You need to be concerned when certain ones occur frequently or when many occur at the same time.

How will you know when the stress level is too high? How can you tell whether the latest slammed door is a natural reaction to a bad day or a symptom of more serious stress? One way is to *keep track of the frequency and intensity of the stress symptoms.* For example, your child may get a headache on occasion, but when your child frequently complains of having a headache, it's time to heed the warning signs. You might also ask your child's teacher, school nurse, or counselor if she or he notices marked changes. If anyone has, consult your family doctor or pediatrician to discuss these changes and the best ways to deal with them.

Keeping a Daily Log

The following *daily log* allows you to note when your children are feeling stress-related symptoms, such as headaches or muscular tension, and how severe or intense these symptoms are. If your children are old enough, they may be able to fill out this log themselves. However, for most children, it is the parent who will complete the log. Keep a running log for seven consecutive days. When you notice your child showing the effects of stress, make a note on the chart about the time of day the symptom began. Symptoms may be indirect, showing up as wincing from a headache, slamming a door from increased irritability, moving awkwardly from stiff muscles, or many other physical manifestations. Your child may also tell you point-blank that he is worried or feeling stressed-out about something.

Make a mark on the daily log, then rate the intensity of the pain or discomfort on a scale of 1 (very weak) to 10 (very strong). Throughout the day, keep charting the different intensity levels. For example, you may notice your child's headache is severe in the early evening but gone shortly before bedtime. Connect each intensity mark to the next hour's mark with a straight line to make a line graph. Label each line graph according to the symptom it records. For example, you may have lines labeled "tantrum," "headache," "sleeplessness."

Some symptoms are high-intensity but short-lived. Put a mark above the time the symptom occurred at the approximate intensity level and label it appropriately. Dizziness or quickened heart rate are examples of short-duration symptoms.

It is important also to note to what degree the stress symptoms interfere with your child's ability to function normally. Indicate next to each time and intensity level the extent to which the symptom impairs the child's daily routine. Use a scale of 1 to 100, with 1 representing no interference at all and 100 indicating total incapacity. Consider such things as the child's ability to concentrate, memory function, the capacity to learn new information, decision-making skills, logic, time management, social interaction, and overall performance. For example, a child may have a severe headache that starts at 10:00 A.M. and gradually lessens in intensity until it is gone at about noon. For the first half-hour, the child has about a 75 percent inability to concentrate or do any of his normal activities. Within an hour, he is back to 50 percent capacity, etc. Try to keep a log both on days that are normal and on days that have something different about them, be it family stress or personal fulfillment.

Below the chart are eight categories. Their purpose is to help you determine whether there were any special events—both

Monday Daily Log

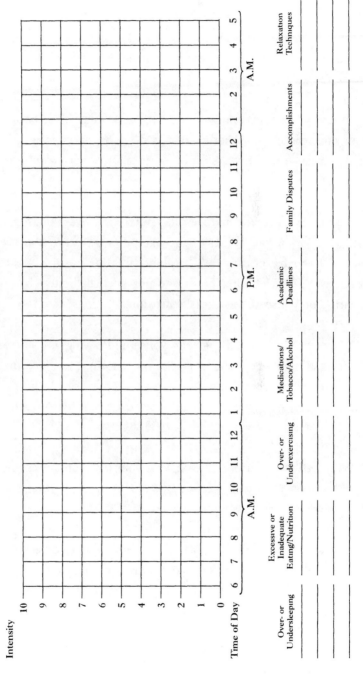

Intensity

10
9
8
7
6
5
4
3
2
1
0

Time of Day

6 7 8 9 10 11 12 1 2 3 4 5 6 7 8 9 10 11 12 1 2 3 4 5

A.M.   P.M.   A.M.

Over- or
Undersleeping

Excessive or
Inadequate
Eating/Nutrition

Over- or
Underexercising

Medications/
Tobacco/Alcohol

Academic
Deadlines

Family Disputes

Accomplishments

Relaxation
Techniques

negative and positive—that made a particular day different from usual. The categories are:

1. **Over- or undersleeping.** Fill in here the number of hours your child slept, and whether that is more or less than usual. A disturbance in normal sleeping patterns is a very common sign of stress.

2. **Excessive or inadequate eating/nutrition.** Was anything different about your child's eating habits on this day? Did he or she have leftover candy for breakfast? Did he or she not eat breakfast? Note whether he or she got normal, better-than-normal, or worse-than-normal nutrition for this day.

3. **Over- or underexercising.** Did your child have gymnastics, or football practice? Did she skip her normal swim team practice and sit around the house watching television? Did he skateboard with friends? Note any divergence from the amount of activity your child normally gets.

4. **Medications/tobacco/alcohol.** Was your child on any medications today? To your knowledge, did he manage to sneak a cigarette or have a drink?

5. **Academic deadlines.** Was there something especially stressful at school today, such as a quiz, or a paper or large homework assignment due?

6. **Family disputes.** Did something happen in the family to cause stress? Did the child have an argument with you or

with his siblings (don't count the normal bickering that goes on daily)? Were there problems with other family members or arguments between the parents and another sibling?

7. Accomplishments. Were there special accomplishments on this day, things that made your child feel particularly good about himself? Were some deadlines met that relieved pressure? Did *you* have a particularly good day and give extra affection and praise to your child?

8. Relaxation techniques. Did your child consciously do anything to make himself feel more relaxed? For example, did he sit quietly and read a book, spend extra time with a best friend, or do yoga in a corner?

The purpose of a chart like this is to give you a picture of when your child's stress occurs and how severe it is. The more you understand about your child's stress, the better you will be able to help him learn to cope with it.

Suicide: The Darkest Side of Stress

Obviously, suicide is not a normal reaction to stress. It is a cry of despair. Every 83 minutes in the United States, a child commits suicide. Each year 500,000—that's *half a million*—children attempt suicide and nearly 300,000 others at least contemplate ending their lives. Since 1965, the incidence of reported suicide among young people has increased more than 300 percent. Suicide now ranks as the third leading cause of death for adolescents, more common than deaths from disease or from alcohol and drug use. And it might be even worse than we think: Although car crashes are the method most often used by older youths to commit suicide, they are not reflected in the above figures.

Nearly all parents of children who have committed, or tried to commit, suicide are initially surprised. "If only I had known" is a common lament. Suicide in children seems so unlikely. What could cause a child to want to end his or her life?

A young person who frequently feels lonely and alienated and who is uncertain what to do about it is at the highest risk for committing suicide. Another at-risk child may experience intense emotional strain, such as being pressured to be excellent in scholastics but secretly feeling unable to live up to high expectations. Or a young person may have had a very negative personal experience in reaching out to the adults in his or her own family. Worse, the child may have been a victim of violence or physical or sexual abuse. In order to reach out for help the child may have to expose family secrets such as alcoholism, violence, or sexual victimization. The child is often afraid of retaliation or at least of further rejection from other family members. In such a household, whether the child is the direct victim or not, the models of behavior she or he observes are confusing and damaging. The child may be fearful that the assault will continue, or that he or she will become like the perpetrator.

Sometimes a child may have difficulty reaching out to an educator or to other students in school. She may interpret this as being universally disliked, and this attitude further contributes to the child holding her feelings inside. Thus, she receives little, if any support and assistance in resolving her problems. Mounting frustrations can lead to an increasingly intense sense of helplessness and powerlessness to change any situation.

We don't *always* know what triggers the moment of final desperation. Trying to keep their children safe, parents must always be monitoring the behaviors of their children to see that they are consistent with healthy growth and development, and they must be willing to seek assistance when they feel a problem is beyond their ability to handle.

Parents need to become more aware of the effects that a crisis, such as death in the family, divorce, alcohol or drug abuse, or simply repeated rejection and alienation (such as a child's having to move and attend new schools repeatedly) can have on their children. The more we know, the better able we are to understand the intensity of our children's feelings, and therefore to prevent suicide. We need to understand the difference between normal growing pains of our children, normal grumpiness and unhappiness, and the desperate depression that is a scream for help.

Serious Distress Signals

While it is true that suicidal feelings most often develop in a person who is deeply depressed, the fact that a child is depressed does not mean he will become suicidal. Healthy, emotionally secure children can deal with the stressors of daily frustrations and periodic trauma. It is children who perceive themselves as worthless and unlovable who are more apt to find the emotional pain they are experiencing absolutely intolerable, and to make a suicide attempt. Most people who commit suicide give clues to their intentions. The following is a list of danger signals. If you recognize any of these in your child, heed the warning signs. Get your child the help he or she needs, immediately.

DISTRESS SIGNALS

- erratic and drastic changes in school-related activities, such as cutting classes, truancy, or dropping out of previously enjoyed clubs or sports groups

- drastic changes in behavior, such as ignoring appearance (when that was not the case previously) or ignoring or dropping friends who used to be important to your child

- talk of owning guns, other weapons, or poison

- extreme and prolonged emotional states such as feelings of guilt, depression, tension, despondency, or hopelessness; self-criticism, self-destructive thoughts, a total lack of goals or ambitions, or a self-image of being a burden to others

- giving away prized possessions such as clothes, jewelry, games, or other valuables; talking about who should get what (such as which sibling should have his room) "someday"

- sending verbal clues: "Soon, no one will have to worry about me," "Don't worry; I won't be a bother anymore," "You'll be sorry, you just wait and see."

- seeming preoccupied with death—talking about it, reading about it, watching gruesome shows, or shows on death and dying; writing stories or poems dealing with feelings of personal worthlessness or

portraying death or heaven as a desirable place;
drawing pictures that portray morbidity, violence,
or self-destructiveness; inappropriate physical risk-taking

• talking about the suicides of others (especially a family
member) or about his or her own previous suicide
attempt

Some distress signals are very obvious, such as talking about
suicide, but others, such as depression, can be harder to recognize. Take all such signs seriously. Don't assume the situation
will cure itself. Suicide threats or attempts are almost always a
way of asking for help and support. To help assess the severity
of these variables, the following questions should be asked about
any of the above:

• Intensity: How intense are the feelings?
• Duration: How long has this been going on?
• Frequency: How much of the time is the young
person feeling this way?

The intensity, the length of time the emotional state and/or
situation has lasted, and the frequency with which the young
person is dealing with negative feelings within a single day are
valuable indicators as to whether speedy intervention is required.
It is the total picture that needs examination. If a child is feeling
severe tension and self-criticism for good reasons—for instance,
if she has been caught telling a lie or cheating on a school
exam—but appears to have reasonable control over her emotional state, she could benefit from counseling although she may

not exhibit suicidal behavior. Successful prevention means helping your child deal with problems before his coping strategies and/or emotional state have deteriorated to the point where a last-straw event could trigger a suicidal act.

Here are some things you can do in monitoring the health and well-being of your children:

1. Regard all use of drugs or alcohol as a serious problem. A child taking drugs or drinking alcohol is especially vulnerable to depression—these substances almost always exacerbate any emotional pain or duress a child is experiencing, making it seem absolutely intolerable.

2. Allow your child to be honest about how hard it is for her to cope with some of life's experiences. By allowing your child to talk about her tough times, you make it more likely that she will turn to you when she feels unable to cope with the situation fueling her pain, despondency, or depression. Parents must understand how difficult this is for children. We often give children more "space" and privileges when they seem to be doing well, or at least saying that all is well. If they tell us things aren't going so well, we are unlikely to allow them to do more. Ask yourself, "What does my child stand to lose if he admits his vulnerability to me?" Let your children know that they have your unconditional love and acceptance, that they can always count on you for help when everything else in their world seems to be crashing down. Above all, when your children show vulnerability to stress, let them know that your actions are about support and assistance and are not punitive.

3. Take your child's feelings seriously. Children often perceive their problems as bigger than they are. For example, a child's experience of the loss of a friend moving away may seem trivial to an adult dealing with divorce or the loss of a spouse, but for the child, the pain level can be equivalent. Children do not have the backlog of experiences adults do; they have not yet learned that there is light at the end of the tunnel. Listen to how *your child* is feeling, observe her behaviors, and then help her deal with the problem, regardless of how unimportant it may seem to you.

4. *Listen* to the words of your child. Often a child gets accustomed to being talked at, rather than listened to. This fosters defensiveness rather than openness. Keep the lines of communication open to facilitate knowing how your child is faring.

5. Consider family counseling. A suicide attempt, though a personal cry of despair, can echo a whole family's deep need for help. When parents (including stepparents and all others active in the child's parenting and guidance) are able to recognize their role in the child's difficulties and actively work toward reducing family conflict, they lessen the child's feelings of pain and increase his feelings of wellness.

6. Encourage positive action aimed at relieving unhappy or troublesome situations. Depressed children often become apathetic and inactive and, as a result, grow more depressed and withdrawn. A vicious cycle is created. A balanced schedule of work, play, and recreation can help. Exhaustion from vigorous physical exercise helps a person relax, sleep better, and have a more positive outlook on life. Likewise, if home life is a problem, then therapy for the child, the parents, or the family can offer a new beginning, a chance to gain a new perspective on the situation.

Remember, any distress signal should be taken with the utmost seriousness. Should you believe that your child is suicidal, seek help immediately. You can begin by calling your child's school counselor, a school nurse, or a school administrator to get a recommendation for a counselor or psychologist. You might also check the listings in the yellow pages. Additionally, suggestions for learning more about suicide can be found in the resource section of this book. The most important step is to reach out for assistance, immediately.

PART III

"A Child's Play Is His Work"

Chapter 5

THE NATURAL STRESS AND STRAINS OF CHILDHOOD

W hen your children were small, you probably purchased books on parenting to find out what developmental steps children customarily go through, and at what age. You were, no doubt, curious to know when your baby should be able to hold his head up, when your toddler should be able to communicate in complete sentences. You checked the book, sometimes anxiously (Why hasn't my child learned to walk by now?), sometimes boastfully (Little Myron is walking a full four months before the average child can!), to see how your child was progressing. It seemed logical to you that there would be standard growth and development patterns within certain age groups.

As you watched and helped your child through each phase, perhaps you came to the conclusion that just as a particular stage of development is stressful for the parents, it is also stressful for the child. Luckily, much of what occurs in each stage is predictable. By knowing what to expect, parents can lessen their own stress and focus on helping their children cope with the inevitable stress they experience.

The Biological Clock of Childhood

When asked, "When will a child learn to walk, to talk, to ride a bicycle?" child development expert Dr. A. Gesell replied, "Not until the cortical development required for the task is completed. Then, and not until then." It seems that the fine coordination necessary for walking, for talking, or for riding a bicycle is difficult, if not impossible, before the motor cortex and cerebellum coordinate certain movements, especially those necessary to keep one's balance. Gesell's work postulates that children's development occurs at intervals. When one kind of growth is accelerated, another is slowed, and as a child progresses to more and more complex behaviors, regression may occur in other areas. For example, as children become preoccupied with speech, a sharp regression in their motor development occurs.

Gesell was so impressed by the *predictability* of the maturation process that he gave little credence to learning as an important factor in behavioral change. This is not to say that environmental influences are not important. Maturational changes influence much of a child's behavior during the first years of life.

It's not only physical development that appears to be time-clock driven. More and more experts recognize that other types of growth may be too. In *touchpoints*, an excellent book for parents of children up to age six, renowned pediatrician and early-childhood-development expert T. Berry Brazelton, M.D., discusses the natural and predictable spurts and regressions that young children go through in different stages of *behavioral* and *emotional* development. Drawing on his more than 40 years of pediatric practice, Dr. Brazelton emphasizes that much of the stress of parenting results from *psychological* growth because new growth in one area may be accompanied by a regression in another, disrupting not only the child but the entire family. Parents who are aware of these stages have a map to the development of their children, a blueprint that can help them understand their children as individuals. Brazelton believes that many parents exacerbate stress in their children as well as themselves because they often meet regression with an attempt to control the behavior, thus foiling the children's efforts at independence.

Parents are more likely to avoid this conflict, and its accompanying stress, when they are aware of certain stages in the growth and development of their children. This chapter provides an overview and is by no means a thorough treatment of the extraordinary developments of childhood. For more information you may want to refer to *touchpoints* (for parents of children from birth to age six), my *Safeguarding Your Teenager from the Dragons of Life* (for the early and later adolescent years), and other resources that are listed in the reference section of this book. Having a general idea of the stages that your children go through at various ages can help you to better understand the accompanying stresses (and understanding helps reduce *your* stress, as well). You can anticipate the stresses and prepare children to cope with them when they arise.

Development through the Years

Childhood is not just about a child getting bigger and better. It's about the miraculous unfolding of a series of phases and stages of development, and the child trying on new capacities. Some of these are the result of the child's biological clock, others are made possible by his interaction with those around him, and still other developments come from his own achievement and mastery (such as learning to hold a spoon, ride a bike, pass a difficult exam). Childhood is a lot of work.

There is a deliberateness about a child's "work." Through his or her actions, a child gains information about himself and the world around him. This is true whether the child is two or twelve or seventeen. A child often knows what he is really up to. For example, a child who has thrown a tantrum of one sort or another will invariably (in his own words) ask the parent, "Do you still love me?" "Am I being good now?" or "Watch me, I am going to be good for you now." The less praise or credit a child deserves, the more he wants and needs it; the very difficult child needs a great deal of assurance.

A child's work at each age is pretty well defined. Each stage of a child's development presents its own set of tasks and demands; all engender internal tension and external stress. This is called "normative" stress because of its predictable occurrence. When parents have a general idea of what behavior is common for their child at these times, they can be less fearful and more effective in their parenting efforts. For example, an eighteen-month-old may undergo episodes of nightwalking as a result of new stresses, such as a fight in play group or a visit to Grandmother's. These are considered "normative," or normal, customary stresses. While there is really no way to prevent the stress, parents who have a general idea of what stresses are customary for children of certain age groups find it easier to identify abnormal or excessive stress. The following material gives a breakdown of the *primary* stresses by age group. Use these guidelines to get a general idea of what stress patterns may be expected.

Birth to Age One

1. Learning cause and effect. Just when parents think they have sorted out the different types of crying babies do (hunger, fatigue, boredom, and discomfort), children start fussing for reasons parents can't fathom—long after their immediate needs have been met. It's easy for parents to become frustrated and pass their stress and frustration on to the baby. Babies do experience stresses we can neither understand nor alleviate—baby frustrations. Though parents should not accept constant fussiness until all preventable sources of stress have been ruled out, they can take comfort in knowing that from time to time, it's normal for regular fussing to continue throughout the day, despite their ministrations.

2. Developing motor skills. At this age, children work hard to sit up straight and to stand up, always looking at their parents for approval. They can become frustrated when their bodies don't respond to their intentions. This is especially noticeable with children on their bellies who accidentally push themselves away from their goals rather than toward them.

3. Recognizing strangers. Children during this time begin to distinguish loved ones from newcomers. Strangers can provide children with too many new and unfamiliar stimuli. Children need time to process each new sight and sound and can become truly upset if someone rushes toward them.

4. Child care/day care stresses. Infancy is an important time for bonding. For the baby, the loving touch and soothing tones of adults—the mother in particular—are vital to physical and emotional growth. The child has had nine months of prenatal time with the mother, and closeness must not be sacrificed, especially when the child is in the care of others. The child wants and needs a great deal of physical touching and emotional soothing and is stressed when it is not forthcoming.

Age Two

1. Establishing separateness. The primary stress facing a child at the age of two is that of establishing separateness, a feeling of being an individual in his own right. Up until this time, he has viewed himself primarily as part of his mother or father, or of the primary caretaker or guardian. At the age of two, the child realizes that he is in reality a separate being. He experiences the stress of developing his own sense of self, of finding power and identifying safe ways to be assertive. He may shout, "Me!" or "Mine!" This can place stress on the parent who until now has had a more dependent and parent-pleasing little child.

2. Making independent choices. Another normative stress occurs when the child finds himself faced with choices that have to be made. Previously, mother or father made all the decisions (what to wear, to eat, to play). Now, *he* has to—wants to—choose his own clothing, which toy he wants to play with. He decides which book he wants to have read to him. Having this newfound power and responsibility can be exhilarating and demanding—and stressful. Parents need to guide their child in the right direction while not completely taking over.

3. Physical and emotional safety. The two-year-old is very physically active, getting into everything, running around. The family needs to keep an eye on him constantly to make sure he doesn't stray out of sight or get hurt. This is exhausting for the caregiver. Most important in this period is staying connected and helping your child recognize that he is a person in his own right; that "separate" feelings are all right. Especially important is allowing your child the feeling that he is being good, doing right, and winning your approval.

4. Establishing gender identification. Children at this age learn to identify with the same-sex parent: boys with their fathers, girls with their mothers. They learn the differences between the genders and first become aware of their sexuality. There may be stress when the child finds out he is not the same as a loved parent.

5. Child care/day care stresses. Perhaps the biggest child care/day care stressor for this age has to do with the child's need for constant monitoring of emotional development. This is an important stage for the child to learn not only what he or she can or cannot touch, or do, or say, but also how he can control and manage his temper and himself in appropriate ways. Much of the adult's time is spent helping the two-year-old learn inner self-discipline. Because the child needs repeated and consistent reinforcement in what the parents wish for him to learn, the child care provider must have an approach similar to that of the parents. A child experiences a great deal of frustration and stress when different adults offer very different levels of control (strict versus permissive) or different styles of guidance and discipline.

Age Three

1. Mastery. A child this age seeks to master her environment. She needs to feel successful. She constantly strains to get recognition. "Watch me! Watch me!" Because the child often labors long and tediously to complete even the simplest tasks, the adult audience may become distracted and not pay (in the child's view) sufficient attention.

2. Curiosity. Another stress results from the nearly insatiable curiosity a three-year-old has. "Why, why, why?" she wants to know. She appears to have unlimited vigor in her discovery mode. This desire always to learn more, do more, understand more, puts a strain on the child's emotional and mental well-being. Parents may not enjoy answering repeated questions, especially when the child's attention span is so short that she is launching the next question before the first one is answered, but it is stressful for her if she is not taken seriously.

3. Monitoring toilet habits. At this age, children may be toilet trained, at least during the daytime. Mistakes (wetting or soiling) are taken as failures by the children. Correction and guidance must be handled carefully to avoid overwhelming children and making them feel as if they have disappointed their parents. Children who have toilet accidents may face the stress of feeling inadequate.

4. Child care/day care stresses. The three-year-old is demanding and expresses a strong resistance to many things the adult requires. The child spends a great deal of energy resisting the adult, whom the child still sees as all-powerful. Withdrawn and insecure much of the time, the child vies for a bit of that power. As a result, one of the biggest challenges to the child care provider is offering the child some power, but not so much that the child believes she wields it all. In doing so, the child care provider must coordinate with the parents to insure that his or her own actions are consistent with that of the parents. The three-year-old, in particular, needs firm and consistent messages about what is and is not acceptable behavior. These messages should be delivered in a way that does not negate her sense of self nor undermine her self-esteem.

Age Four

1. Developing fears and phobias. The four-year-old's world is rapidly expanding. She may develop fears of noisy things such as fire engine sirens or barking dogs. She may become concerned with broader issues, such as the other children in the neighborhood, suddenly becoming afraid of ones with whom she had previously coexisted peacefully.

2. Controlling unwanted feelings. Four-year-olds find themselves full of feelings that frighten them, feelings they think they should not have. For example, a child who has already come to terms with the new baby in the household may suddenly find the rivalry heating up again. Her aggressive feelings frighten her and take a strong effort to control. She is doubly stressed, first by the rudimentary guilt or shame she feels at having such feelings, and second by the effort it takes to control them.

3. Needing the approval of peers. At this age, children begin to place more importance on relationships with others of the same age. They need peer experiences. They tease each other, make each other angry, and hug and kiss each other. They develop exaggerated senses of loving and hating their friends, kissing and cuddling one minute, striking out the next. They wish to be accepted as part of the group.

4. Trying out new behaviors. This is a year of exploration. Children may develop new behaviors, such as lying, stealing, and masturbating. They go through a pattern, trying something out and then moving on to the next idea. These new behaviors are stressful because they may bring about parental disapproval. Parents who are concerned about the actions will pressure the children to stop, confusing them or adding to the tension. The children may respond by rebelling and continuing the action until it becomes a habit, causing additional friction between the child and the parents.

5. Child care/day care stresses. The four-year-old is a very loving child who wants to please her parents and all adults she knows. Because of this, it's very important the day care/ child care provider be a warm and accessible person, one who is willing to nurture and provide emotional comfort and closeness. When it is not forthcoming, the four-year-old easily becomes sad, despondent, and tearful. Adult closeness can alleviate stress for this child; conversely, when adult closeness is withheld, it can be a real source of stress for the four-year-old.

Age Five

1. Pleasing others. The primary stress is the need to please the mother, the most important person in the child's world. Having matured from the totally self-centered two-year-old, a five-year-old wants to be near his mother, to talk with her, play with her, help her, gain her approval. In his determination to please his mother (or father, if the father is the primary caretaker), the child works extremely hard to "do the right thing," something that is stressful at any age. A five-year-old will ask permission for even the most minor things. This can become annoying and stressful for the parents, who often snap back with comments like, "Don't keep asking me if you can have a glass of water! You know you can have a glass of water whenever you want one!" In addition, the parent often has to be extremely careful of the five-year-old's feelings, which are easily hurt. If a mother snaps at her son, he is likely to cry, feeling he has done something terribly wrong in the eyes of the person he loves the most. Hearing her son cry after being snapped at makes the mother feel guilty. The near-obsession the child has with the mother creates an emotional strain for both mother and child, causing many parents to wonder if they really should go back to work, or to feel guilty if and when they do.

2. Separation anxiety. The five-year-old can be terrified if his mother is out of his sight for even a minute. He clings to her, needs to be within sight of her, within the sound of her voice. When she leaves, such as to go out to dinner with her husband, the strain in the child is physical and emotional. He is not quite certain that nothing will happen to his beloved mother and fears that she might never come back. Parents heading out for a night on the town to relax may become stressed as they feel guilty for leaving their child behind.

3. School stresses. Most of the fears that a five-year-old encounters have to do with the safety of his parents and with issues of abandonment. He worries that his parents may die or be hurt while he is away at school, or that they will not return to the school to pick him up at the end of the day. The educator and the parent must constantly reassure the child that the parent will be safe at home or at work and, of course, that she or he will return at the end of the school day to pick up the child.

Age Six

1. Becoming self-centered. At age six, the main stress on a child is the process of becoming more self-centered, shifting the focus of his world from his parents to himself. He is attempting to identify his own interests, to make himself a separate individual. He may be under strain as he flits from one interest to another, trying as many things as possible in order to find out what "fits." At this age, the child places a great deal of stress on the family, as well. He disrupts the peace by constantly boasting about what he can do, or by asserting his independence in small but annoying ways, such as refusing to sit in his regular chair at the dinner table, insisting on sitting where *he* wants to sit, not where you've told him to sit.

2. Testing newfound independence. This child is always testing his newfound independence, always testing to see where the boundaries are. Parents often worry that they are losing control of their child, that he no longer listens and minds as he should. They feel they are constantly scolding the child, always disciplining him. The loving days of the clinging five-year-old are remembered nostalgically.

3. School stresses. The first-grader is fearful of being hit by another student, worries that he may wet himself in class and that the other students will make fun of him because of it, and is frightened by the large and noisy school bus. Helping the child feel comfortable about asking to use the restroom when necessary can alleviate the fear of wetting himself. Providing adults to monitor playground activities will reduce his chance of being hit. Taking the first-grader to the bus and meeting it later will also ease his fears.

Ages Seven and Eight

1. Coping with a need for acceptance. Children at this age particularly want to be liked and appreciated by their parents and by their teachers. They strive to be the teacher's pet, without being obvious enough about it to be ridiculed by their peers. They face the stress of feeling rejected when the teacher calls on another child to clean the blackboard, or when the parent praises a sibling instead.

2. Trying to accomplish more. As the child at this age becomes more independent, he takes on more and more tasks and begins to worry that he will not have enough time to finish them. He may become so pressured that he drops all of the tasks, then hears from his parents about being irresponsible. He becomes frustrated because he wants to do so much but can't quite manage his time wisely. He is not yet mature enough to understand his own limits.

3. Self-consciousness. Seven- and eight-year-olds have a fear of being singled out. They are self-conscious and easily embarrassed. Ask a seven-year-old to stay after school and she may be horrified. If a teacher makes an example of the child, to make a point for the rest of the class, the child may become so stressed she doesn't want to go to school the next day. Alienation is a major stressor at this age.

4. School stresses. Second- and third-grade students are most fearful of not being able to do something well in class, such as spelling words on a quiz correctly, or passing a test. This child is also fearful of the teacher's discipline. He wants to be asked to be the teacher's helper and considers this to be a sign of being liked by the teacher. He feels very strongly about being scolded by his teacher, interpreting this as a sign that the teacher does not like him.

Ages Nine and Ten

1. Sexual identification. Children are still sorting out their feelings regarding the opposite sex. Boys may want to avoid girls, remaining only with other boys, while the more mature girls may begin to look for boyfriends. This places stress on both sexes—the boys who are trying to avoid the girls, and the girls who are wondering why the boys always avoid them.

2. Increased dependence on special friends. Best friends are critical now. Children have one or two close friends to whom they tell all their secrets, with whom they have extremely close emotional bonds. They worry constantly about losing their best friend's affection and respect. They are very concerned with their image in the eyes of their best friend, thinking more about how something will affect the friend than how it will affect themselves and their families.

3. Appearance anxiety. Appearance is now beginning to be important, especially to girls. Children begin to form cliques based on appearance: the prettiest girls, the cutest boys. Children may experiment with their appearance, dressing conservatively one day, more expressively the next. If their appearance does not match that of the group to which they belong, this will cause stress. For example, overweight children may become especially sensitive to slurs about their weight and want to slim down to fit in with the cool crowd.

4. School stress. The fourth- and fifth-grade child's bigger fears revolve around friendships. This child fears that a school friend will betray her by choosing a new friend or by sharing a guarded secret—*their* secret—with someone else. Helping a child evaluate why a particular boy or girl is his friend can help him be more objective in making multiple friendships. At this age you want your children to learn the art of team play and team spirit.

Age Eleven

1. Sexual insecurity. An eleven-year-old is beginning to hear all sorts of wild stories as to what sex really is and what people do in bed. He doesn't know enough yet to separate fact from fiction, and he readily exchanges the wildest stories with his peers. He may begin to feel pressure to experiment sexually, and he may brave the gentler acts such as hand holding and slight kissing. He doesn't know what the members of the opposite sex expect from him, and, lacking a solidly formed identity, he is rarely able to talk openly and candidly about sexual issues.

2. Experimenting with emotional stress. Every little mood swing becomes exaggerated. Eleven-year-olds are experimenting with moods and finding their own personalities. They are self-centered, fretting for hours over their own emotional states.

3. Popularity anxiety. When children of this age do think about others, it is usually only to worry about how those others view them. "Am I popular?" is the biggest topic of thought and conversation.

4. Body consciousness. Eleven-year-olds, especially the more sexually developed girls, begin to become very concerned with exposing their bodies. They worry about gym class, for which they must disrobe in front of others, take communal showers, and let others see them naked. Breasts and pubic hair can be a source of extreme embarrassment. Children worry that they are over- or underdeveloped in comparison to their peers. They often want to avoid gym class or any other activity (such as swimming) that makes them show their bodies.

5. School stress. The sixth-grader feels insecure about his appearance and fears that peers will mock the way he looks. This is also the age of concern about the developing body, mostly because the child doesn't understand what is going on, nor can he quite understand his emotional ups and downs. Since his classmates and friends are also in a state of disarray, the child tries especially hard to not alienate the important adults in his life, so parents and educators generally find the relationship with this child easy going.

Ages Twelve and Thirteen

1. Intense physical growth and development. The preteen and teen find that their bodies are going through incredible physical changes. They gain more weight, height, heart size, lung capacity, and muscular strength than in the previous four years of development. Bone growth exceeds muscle development, generally resulting in poor coordination. The children feel clumsy and awkward. Body contours change as well, and not always in ways the children view as positive. Noses may elongate and thicken, ears protrude, arms lengthen. The bodily changes lead to mental and emotional stress as the children wonder what they will look like when they finally "settle into" their bodies. At this age, girls often grow faster and mature more rapidly than boys. For the next two years, girls will be about two to four inches taller than boys.

2. Sexual maturation. The differences in physical development between same-age, different-sex children create anxiety for the youngsters. At the same time, these children have to deal with the body's readying itself for sexual reproduction. This stage of puberty produces some of the most dramatic sexual changes in the children's lives: the growth of pubic hair, the development of breasts, the onset of menstruation, the ability to have erections and nocturnal emissions (wet dreams), and the discovery of arousal through manipulation (masturbation). Children undergoing these sexual changes are often confused, and they suffer mental and emotional stress along with the physical.

3. School stress. Seventh- and eighth-grade children fear being selected first (and having to lead) or last (which makes them feel disliked or unpopular). They also fear the mysteries of their rapidly developing sexuality (peers have shared wild stories or myths) and do not like to be criticized about their appearance. Because of this, they often balk at participating in activities that require exposure of the body, such as having to take a group shower after gym class. This is also an age at which the child begins to worry about his happiness or unhappiness. Because he is emotionally fragile, this is the age of easy sulking.

Ages Fourteen and Fifteen

1. Growing pains. The children of this age group are experiencing growth spurts that can leave them tired and hungry. They have "growing pains" they swear they can feel, including joint pains and headaches. These physical ailments place a great strain on the body, of course, but they also leave the children feeling mentally stressed, wondering what is going to happen to them next.

2. Raging hormones. With the onset of sexual maturity and the surge in hormones, fourteen-year-olds begin to experience sexual desires. If they have not been taught about sex and reproduction, they may be highly confused and suffer from feelings of guilt.

The raging hormones produce erratic behavior. Children are at one moment prone to inferiority, anxiety, and fear and then shift to periods of bravado and superiority. They are easily offended (causing stress for other family members, who have to walk on eggshells in order to avoid making a scene) and highly sensitive to criticism. They exaggerate simple occurrences and believe that their problems, experiences, and feelings are unique to themselves. This feeling of being all alone, of being the only one who has ever had to go through all this, creates a great deal of stress for the children in this age group.

3. Jealousy. At this age, children can be jealous of anyone and anything that prevents them from being with their friends or sweethearts. LaVonne worries that Marcie is spending more time with Tina than with her. Martin becomes concerned when LaVonne even looks at another boy, certain he is going to lose her. The jealousy can be unfounded and irrational, but it's very real. If the jealousy in fact has a cause, if the friend or sweetheart does leave for another, the stress is doubled.

4. School stress. The ninth- and tenth-grader also has great bouts of insecurity about her sexuality and balks at activities that require exposure of the body. This child is acutely aware of her happiness and unhappiness, and because hormones are causing mood swings, she sometimes fears she is "going crazy." This is the age of learning about the boundaries of love, and so this child fears that a peer will vie for her sweetheart. Boys do not want to be challenged, but frequently they are. Both boys and girls fear a confrontation or fight over a boyfriend/girlfriend. The classic fear of being disliked or unpopular is ever present. Now aware of becoming an adult, this child looks intently to parents, educators, and other adults in her life to see how they experience adulthood. Because all adults, especially her parents, are important in her efforts to find out what it is like to be an adult, she closely observes adults. Because she is ever ready to speak her mind and to challenge, both educators and parents find this child "sassy."

Ages Sixteen and Seventeen

1. Facing the world. The child of this age worries about getting a car, taking college entrance exams, having to make decisions about what to do with the rest of her life. Suddenly, the question "What do you want to be when you grow up?" has to be answered seriously. This is a time of confusion and uncertainty. There is duality in these teenagers, a physical and emotional jumble, hindered by an inability to look ahead and visualize the long-term effects of present behaviors. Today, right now, is all that matters. Feelings of invulnerability and immortality lead teenagers to act in reckless ways: to drive too fast, experiment with drugs, have unsafe sex. This is a time of identity crisis, a time between dependent (and safe) childhood and independent (and frightening) adulthood.

2. Physical maturity. Some children at this age are still going through the physical strains of growth, especially boys, who often have their growth spurts later than girls. Sexuality and feelings of desire fight with what the children have learned about responsibility and abstinence. There is a great deal of stress caused by the conflict between what they learned from their parents, what their bodies are telling them to do now, and the conflicting messages society sends them.

3. Ancient parents. There is also stress, on both the child and her family, stemming from the teenager's new attitude toward her parents. She finds them hopelessly naive and old fashioned. She pities them for their out-of-date ideas and assumes an attitude of superiority that can be quite annoying to the parents. She may constantly challenge the household rules, seeking in small ways to assert her independence. She is fiercely loyal to peer group values, which may be different from the values of her family. Since children at this age often reinvent themselves again and again, the parent faces the shock of coming home and finding a stranger at the dinner table. Something the parent said to her child just a few weeks ago may trigger scorn and derision now.

4. School stress. While the sixteen- and seventeen-year-old child worries whether she meets the expectations of her peers in looking the way she is supposed to, her bigger fears have to do with adult authority. A high school junior or senior feels a sense of independence and does not want adults to make her decisions for her, nor prescribe roles. Especially bothersome for this child is not knowing what to do in terms of work. This triggers her unrest at not being more successful in school efforts ("I'm not a good student"; "I don't do well in school").

Age Eighteen

1. Life decisions. Many children have finished their primary growth spurt by eighteen. They are feeling more comfortable with their bodies. Now the chief cause of stress is the need to make adult, long-term, life-changing decisions. An eighteen-year-old has to develop her own values, to decide which ones to keep and which to discard. (The strain on a family is intense if the child chooses to discard an integral family value. A prime example of this is the child who decides to go outside the family religion, or to drop religion entirely.) She has to develop a meaningful and workable philosophy of life. She reevaluates her morality, searching for her own personal convictions.

There are many social strains at this time. The child is graduating from high school, leaving the comfortable environment that has been his life. He no longer can define himself in the role of "high school student" or as a member of a high school peer group. Friendships may be lost as children scatter to colleges throughout the country. Children may measure themselves against their friends, seeing who got into the "best" colleges, and be stressed over finding themselves less than adequate in their own eyes.

2. Independence. Another main stress at this time is the very real fact of independence, both physical and mental. Over the previous few years, the child has been *attempting* to assert his independence—to dress differently, to challenge household rules. But now, as the child prepares to go to college or move out on his own, he finds that he is independent in fact, not just in desire. He may have to be financially responsible, handling his own checking account, paying his bills. With no parent around to remind him of things that need to be done or deadlines to be met, he will have to take care of himself.

3. School stress. For the eighteen-year-old, the primary concern stems from his desire to clarify for himself what is appropriate in terms of values, goals, relationships, and choices of what to do and where to go. Personal needs become important ("What will I do for a job, career, college, training?"), and he fears that he has not taken his role as a learner seriously ("I just didn't take school seriously"; "I don't think I learned anything"; "I don't think I'll make it in college"; "I don't have any idea what I am good at doing").

It can be helpful to understand the stresses our children experience that are unique to their stage of development, and how the inherent tasks and demands of being that age are stressors. Understanding allows you to avoid adding to the stress you or your child is feeling, and helps your child learn ways to deal with the stress he is undergoing. When your five-year-old clings to you, you know that doing so is normal and that it is not a sign of stunted emotional independence. When a fourteen-year-old believes that teenagers have all the answers and that adults are the cause of the problems in his life, you can reassure yourself that it is a normal sign of your child's growing independence and is typical of his age group.

Stay tuned to the stress and strains of childhood. Talk to other parents about the stages their children are in, the things they (children and parents alike) have gone through. Watch closely for stress signs that indicate your child is not coping well, and then get help if you feel you need it in order to assist your child. School counselors, your family doctor, and your child's pediatrician are all potential sources of help.

Chapter 6

STRESS AT SCHOOL

Eighty percent of the time, learning difficulties are related to stress.
Remove the stress and you remove the difficulties.
—GORDON STOKES

Jackson tells the story of the time he came home exhausted from work and plopped into a chair. As he was having a beer, his nine-year-old son came in and, mimicking his father, flopped into a chair, sighing. As Jackson and his wife watched, little Bob held a cold soda can against his forehead, slumped in the chair, and proclaimed, "I have had such a stressful day today. The teacher was on my case, my friends were all stressed out over the big test, and I'm totally exhausted." Jackson's son was doing the exact same thing that Jackson often did at the end of a long day at the office. Like father, like son; like office stress, like school stress.

School Stress #1: The Art of Being a Student

Just as you go to work every day, your children go to school every day. Going to school, getting an education, is their "job." They spend nearly as many hours a day at school as you do at work, and they almost certainly put in as many, if not more, homework hours than you do. While you have cultivated some friends from your work, nearly all of your children's friends are from school. Some of your social activities might be decreed by your job, such as Christmas parties, baby showers, retirement get-togethers and the like; virtually every social outing your children have is tied to school. In other words, while your job is an important part of your life, your children's job of going to school is a central part of theirs, second only to their home and family and neighborhood.

School Stress #2: Personal Safety

There are various types of stresses your children may encounter at school that you yourself don't have to deal with at your job, or which you may not have even thought of. One of the most critical stresses in school is a concern you and I probably never had there—a concern for physical safety. When we went to school our biggest fears were likely that the big kids would try to take away our milk money, or that we would be punched on the bus or sneered at by bullies. Those bullies have grown up and had children of their own, who have taken their parents' childhood antics a quantum leap forward, to harsh swearwords, brass knuckles, knives, and even guns.

Of course, not everyone has had the same experience. When

I went to school in a small farm community, we were told that in the inner city, kids were having sex at ages nine and ten, drugs were everywhere, and youngsters were stabbing one another. Even way back in my school days, some places were more dangerous than others. However, for most of us, school safety was not as great a concern in our time as it is today.

Student violence escalates every year. Common incidents of such violence include verbal and physical threats, and robbery by force. Assault and injury can be severe, even deadly. Disgruntled students who have problems in their homes and neighborhoods bring those problems to school and take them out on their innocent classmates. Children who are hit and abused by their parents stalk the hallways, preying on smaller children. Students who feel that they have been humiliated by teachers but are afraid to take on the authority figure will take out their aggressions on other children, often on the "eggheads" who are seen as teachers' pets. The stereotype of the class nerd genius who can't stand up for himself and gets pushed into a locker has been rewritten: The child is still a nerd, but instead of getting a simple noogie on the head or being stuffed into a locker, that hapless child is now knifed, beaten, sometimes murdered. The six o'clock news has examples every month.

Gangs are posing a growing threat as well. Many schools now forbid children to wear certain colors or clothing (such as Oakland Raiders jackets) associated with gang membership. Students who don't want to join gangs may find that they have no choice. The "If you're not with us, you're against us" mentality is at work. It's not only the big kids who hang out; the gang tentacles extend as far as elementary school. And don't think your daughters are safe just because they happen to be female.

More and more girls are joining—or being forced to join—gangs, gangs that often are at least as violent as the male gangs. It wasn't so long ago that there was a report in the news of a particularly vicious initiation rite that would-be girl gang members had to go through. To prove their bravery, they had to have sex unprotected with a male gang member who was known to be HIV-positive. They were risking their lives to get into the gang.

The statistics bear sad witness to these problems. According to a recent *U.S. News & World Report* "Violence in School" study, more than three million crimes a year are committed in or near the eighty-five thousand public schools in the U.S., costing taxpayers nearly sixty million dollars. Of special concern is that "school crimes have grown more violent, the perpetrators steadily younger." Nearly 9 percent of eighth-graders carry a gun, knife, or club to school at least once a month, and an "estimated 270,000 guns go to school every day."

The extent of criminal activity *each month* in America's secondary schools is staggering. In a typical month:

- 2.4 million students have personal property stolen,
- 112,000 students are robbed through force, a show of weapons, or threats,
- 282,000 students are physically attacked,
- 800,000 students stay home because they are afraid to go to school.

And it isn't only the students who are encountering problems. Teachers are exposed to physical threats and assaults as well.

Each month 6,000 teachers are robbed and 1,000 teachers are assaulted seriously enough to require medical attention. In addition, *each month* more than 125,000 teachers encounter at least one situation in which they are afraid to confront misbehaving students. How safe can a child feel when she sees that even the adult, the teacher, is not safe?

Deteriorating, Toxic, and Crowded Facilities

In addition, our children often worry about threats to their physical safety at school from sources *other than* violent students. These safety problems can be caused by buildings that are falling apart; worn-out desks, lockers, and bookcases; toxic substances that leak into the air and the ground; and schools that are near sites of drive-by shootings and drug deals. Some schools are near freeways, and the resulting noise and air pollution can give children headaches and cause them stress.

Some children still are bused long distances to school and don't feel comfortable in the neighborhood in which their school is located. Bused children have fewer opportunities to stay after school and participate in sports or club activities. Even worse, bused children are often not accepted by their peers back in the neighborhood when they return home; they are socially penalized for going to a different school.

Perhaps the greatest physical stress in most schools today is caused by overcrowding. Just think of how tense you get when you are doing your last-minute holiday shopping, fighting those huge crowds at the mall. You probably spend a few hours cheek-by-jowl and come home exhausted and stressed out. Children in crowded schools have that same experience day in and day out, with no relief in sight. You at least have the option of leaving the mall at any time and coming back when you know the stores will be less crowded. Children can't leave school whenever they become anxious, and they can't anticipate less crowded situations any time soon. If anything, the school crowding problem is expected to worsen.

Children need a break, even from their peers. No matter how much they enjoy the company of their friends, children need a time to get away and be by themselves. They need downtime. The constant noise, the battle with the crowds in the hallways, the need to perform intelligently for the teachers, the concern over appearance and popularity—all these combine to grind a child down. A teacher can at least take a few minutes to hide out in the teachers' lounge for a little private time. Children have no place they can go to be alone in school.

School Stress #3:
Testing Terror and Performance Anxiety

Many stresses are built into going to school. The most common ones are testing and grades. Every child has to worry constantly about the next test coming up. Just think how you would feel if your self-worth depended on being tested day in and day out. Maybe you get a merit review at work once a year or so and are nervous for days before. Your children have pop quizzes and tests, sometimes every day, and sometimes more than one in a day. And even the most jaded child feels that he is a dummy if he has test scores lower than those of his friends. Sometimes children are not prepared for exams, for reasons ranging from too many hours in extracurricular activities or part-time jobs, to not being able to drag themselves away from the video arcade, to a simple dislike of studying. A lack of preparation is a major cause of stress. Then there is the pressure put on children by their parents. We know our children's potential and expect them to live up to it with every quiz, every exam. Children are aware of their parents' expectations and feel pressured to measure up to them.

Finally, there are some children who have test anxiety. No matter how intelligent they are, no matter how well prepared they are, they simply do not take tests well. Many students feel frustrated that nothing they do seems to help. Teachers often hear the wail "But I *did* study!"

The Seven Intelligences

We are beginning to understand more about the stress of learning and, in particular, about how students learn. Not everyone learns the same way; if you have more than one child, you have probably already noticed this. Perhaps your son picks up anything that is set to music, while your daughter remembers things she sees better than things she hears. School causes stress by treating all children as if they learn in the same way. Most educators emphasize reading ability or linguistic intelligence. Many standardized IQ tests focus on this as well. Yet it is only one of the seven types of intelligence.

According to Harvard psychologist Howard Gardner, the seven intelligences are as follows:

1. **Linguistic intelligence.** This is our ability to read and write, to use words well. Writers, speakers, and politicians develop this type of intelligence. Children who are linguistically intelligent are systematic, enjoying patterns and order.

They have good memories for trivia and enjoy word games. This type of intelligence is highly prized in our school system. Teachers often use stories, vocabulary games, and discussions to teach material. Unfortunately, students who have not developed their linguistic intelligence may be unable to learn via those techniques and as a result may feel confused and stupid.

2. Logical or mathematical intelligence. This ability, most often developed in scientists, mathematicians, and lawyers, is the ability to reason or calculate. Children who have well-developed logical intelligence like to count, to be precise. They are often good at using computers, liking and understanding the orderly basis of programming and application. They enjoy problem solving. Schools also reward students with logical or mathematical intelligence; deductive thinking and computer skills are emphasized in the classroom. Students who do not have this type of intelligence quickly feel left out.

3. Musical intelligence. Composers and conductors and musicians are obviously strong in musical intelligence. Musically intelligent people are often very sensitive to the emotional power of music, aware of its complex organization. They may be deeply spiritual. Cultures that do not have written languages use music to communicate and value musical intelligence. In our society, however, we do not often classify musical ability as intelligence but dismiss it lightly as a "knack" or a "gift." Children who are good at music can reduce the stress of learning by integrating music with other subject areas. They can learn dates and other "have to memorize" material through rap or rhythm. Perhaps most important, children with musical intelligence can use music to help them relax and change their moods. When they are stressed from learning in the "normal" (i.e. linguistic or logical) mode, they have the ability to reframe the material as music that they understand.

4. Spatial or visual intelligence. Architects, sculptors, and pilots test high in this area. A good battlefield strategist would be highly spatially intelligent. Children with this intelligence can remember things well when they are put into picture form; they can memorize maps and charts. They like to see the whole picture all at once, rather than learning in bits and pieces. They use mental images and metaphors for learning. Unfortunately, our schools often present material sequentially, in dribs and drabs, working up to a conclusion. This can frustrate the spatially gifted child who wants to see the whole gestalt first and then come back to flesh out the details.

5. Kinesthetic intelligence. Also called physical intelligence, this is highly developed in athletes, dancers, gymnasts, and surgeons. Kinesthetically intelligent children have good control over their bodies and like to use them, participating in sports, dance, and anything else that requires movement. They have good timing and are highly sensitive to the physical environment. These are children who learn best by doing, by touching, by moving objects around. They are good with models and handicrafts. They become stressed when they are forced to sit still for long, when they must listen but not participate physically.

6. Interpersonal intelligence. "People people" rate high in interpersonal intelligence. They relate well to others. Salespeople, negotiators, motivational speakers, and coaches have high interpersonal intelligence. Children with this intelligence are very social, joining groups, understanding other children, communicating—and even manipulating—quite well. They do excellently in school activities that require partners or teamwork, much less well in situations that demand solo activity. These children become stressed when they can't talk over their projects with others. They need to take breaks to socialize, to keep in touch with the other students.

7. Intrapersonal intelligence. This intelligence is often called intuition. It is the ability to tap into information stored in the subconscious mind. Philosophers, mystics, and counselors show this type of intelligence. Children who have intrapersonal intelligence are very sensitive. They understand themselves well and are self-motivated. They do not do well when teachers spell out every detail of a project, insisting that something be done precisely by the book. Intrapersonal people want to be different, want to use their self-knowledge and develop their own feelings. They have a purpose in life and are aware of their own strengths and weaknesses. In the classroom, they often become upset when they are expected to conform. Teachers who recognize students with intrapersonal intelligence would do well to allow them to be different from the group, or to do independent-study activities. These students learn quickly when they are allowed to take control of their own learning.

No one of these seven intelligences is better than the others. All are good. Children may have more than one kind of intelligence; in fact, most children will be strong in two or three areas. Observe each of your children. It is very likely that their gifts or strengths—the one or two areas in which they find mastery relatively easy—will be very different for each child. Sometimes parents express it best when they say, "My children are all so different." For each of your children, ask, "What are this child's primary and secondary strengths—what are the dominant and secondary intelligences?" We want our children to discover their strengths and then to find enjoyment in excelling in these areas. This is the real reason we parents expose our children to a variety of activities. Once you discover more about your child's intellectual strengths, *encourage* him in what he excels at.

How to Help Your Child Develop His or Her Learning Abilities

Learning is difficult for most students. Often when students do poorly in school, the reason is that they don't know *how* to learn. By strengthening your child's learning abilities, you can help him succeed in school. Children who see themselves learning, achieving, and gaining mastery are less frustrated with themselves. As they begin to feel successful in their endeavors, stress is diminished and their self-esteem increases.

The Amazing Brain

Teachers sometimes joke about the student who showed up for class but forgot to bring a brain. The brain is, of course, an important asset the student needs to bring to class regularly. We parents need to take an active role in helping our child value the brain as the center of his or her education. We now know so much more about the brain than we did even a mere decade ago. Scientists and psychologists have alerted us to new information about this amazing machine and how it functions. We parents can benefit from this new information and teach our children a respect for the brain's role in the learning process. Children who see themselves learning are less frustrated and encounter less stress in their thirteen or so years in their "careers" as students.

The brain is an amazing and powerful computer. Weighing less than three pounds and just bigger than a grapefruit, it is thousands of times more powerful than computers filling whole rooms. It has trillions of cells capable of making connections more numerous than the number of atoms in the entire universe, according to Stanford University professor Robert Ornstein.

The brain has three distinct parts. The first is the lower brain, or brain stem, which controls our involuntary functions. This part regulates breathing and heartbeat. The second-tier brain is just above the brain stem. It deals with emotions. The third part of the brain, the cortex, helps us with our intellectual processes. Only about one-eighth of an inch thick, the cortex has six layers, each with different functions. It is this third part of the brain that makes humans a unique species, capable of learning and progressing.

In education, a stimulated brain functions in three areas: First, it helps students store information quickly, thoroughly, and efficiently. Second, it enables students to solve problems, and third, it allows students to generate new ideas. The brain is dynamic and responds quickly to new stimuli. It can keep improving from birth to old age if it receives sufficient energy. It is the energy that allows students to make the most of their brains, to use their intelligence regardless of which type of intelligence it is.

The brain can be as little as 2 percent of body weight yet use up as much as 20 percent of the body's energy. That's why it is vital to supply the proper foods to maximize that energy. One important energy source is **glucose**, found in fruits and vegetables. **Potassium** and **sodium**, also found in fruits and vegetables, help "pump" information across the brain. Without sufficient potassium, students may feel drowsy or be in a stupor (which has the same root as the word *stupid*). They may vomit or simply feel nauseated, conditions obviously not conducive to learning. **Protein** is also vital for the neurotransmitters that produce the chemical flows across the brain. A sensible diet that includes fresh vegetables, fruit (especially bananas, which are rich in potassium, and oranges, which are full of vitamin C), and protein will keep energy flowing to the brain. Fish and vegetable oils, along with linoleic acid from nuts, help to repair the "insulation" around the brain's message tracks.

There is one more way besides nutrition to supply the brain with energy: **exercise**. The brain needs oxygen. Cut off the oxygen supply for even a little while and the brain dies. You've probably heard of "brain dead" people (for example, children who have been at the bottom of swimming pools, unable to breathe). Their bodies still can function but their brains have shut off due to lack of oxygen. When you exercise, you breathe deeply, taking in more oxygen and supplying the brain with what it needs. Deep breathing oxygenates the blood flowing to the brain. Ever notice how when you are confused about something you stop, shake your head, take a few deep breaths, and feel better able to concentrate? It's the oxygen that's helping.

Helping Our Children Develop Their Learning Abilities

According to the experts Gordon Dryden and Jeanette Vos, authors of *The Learning Revolution*, there are four simple steps we can use to help our children develop their learning abilities.

1. Make learning fun from the beginning. Shapes are all around: The moon is round, the silo is cylindrical, the door is rectangular, the Christmas tree is conical. Numbers are easy to learn when taught in the context of everyday life: one nose, but two ears; two hands, but ten fingers. You want your child to feel that learning is anytime, anywhere, and fun. This principle applies to children of all ages.

2. Encourage movement. Children love to run around, to jump, to push. Even the smallest babies explore; they are preprogrammed to crawl, to walk. Be sure your baby is not so bundled up that she can't move her limbs, or that the playroom is not so full of objects that a small child can't run around freely. Creeping and crawling help your baby develop visual acuity and muscular strength, just as physical activity does for your teenager. "Peak performance" entails the body and mind working in concert. A child is most ready to learn after physical stimulation, especially when it is aerobic in nature. The child coming to the classroom (or sitting down to do homework) after having bicycled to or from school is at his "personal best" and learning best. The same goes for the child who has just come in from playtime (or recess), or a physical education class, or a sports practice—whether it be dance, gymnastics, skateboarding, or football.

3. Develop children's five senses. Children try to touch, smell, taste, hear, and look at everything around them. We can encourage aptitude in these abilities by providing children with a feast for their senses. For example, instead of having plain white walls in a child's room, allow it to be painted or wallpapered with strikingly colored geometric figures. Music helps children develop communication abilities and differentiate sounds. Objects of different sizes, shapes, and textures help them develop an acute sense of touch. When possible, take this into account in decorating your children's rooms or study area (and the family room).

4. Encourage language development at all ages. Don't talk down to your children. Children are able to learn a complete language in three years (foreign children learn fluent English in that time). Speak in full sentences. Use sophisticated words and foreign phrases. Help your children develop good reading skills. Show an interest in learning through reading, and encourage them in reading. Expose your children to books and magazines. Allow each child to subscribe to a magazine that is of interest *to him*. And remember how important modeling is; your children need to see you reading, too.

School Stress #4: Is Your Child Popular Enough?

Another common stress is the pressure to be popular. Being part of a crowd, especially the "in crowd," is a measure of self-worth to children. Children who are not liked or accepted feel left out. Popularity and acceptance may be based on such characteristics as good looks, athletic ability, social grace, religious affiliation, ethnic group membership, and special talents (the most popular child in my daughter's first-grade class could balance a quarter on her nose!). Since many of those characteristics are beyond the control of children, they experience great stress in being unable to change to fit into the groups they perceive as most desirable.

The problems don't end when a child becomes a member of a group. Groups might not expect total conformity (although some gangs will settle for nothing less), but they do expect members to conform to some degree in order to bolster the group. If a member perceives the expectations of peers to be in conflict with his values and needs, group identification becomes more difficult. When such a conflict reaches an intolerable level, the child experiences the acute stress of having to choose between an unhappy, self-imposed continuation of membership, and withdrawal, which is followed by the even more stressful process of seeking membership in an alternative peer group.

Teacher's Pet . . . Or Teacher's Pest?

Teachers often bring up a source of childhood stress that parents might not think of readily: the pressure of the child wanting the teacher to like him. Of course, we know that very small children often congregate around the teacher and want to be her best friend, but even older students care a great deal what the teacher thinks, no matter what the students say. Just as a parent may find one of her children more difficult to like than the others, educators don't necessarily like all students equally. The goal for teachers is to act professionally and not let their personal feelings and emotions affect the way they treat students, but realistically, some of those feelings are bound to be sensed. It is particularly bad when a teacher is of one ethnic group and appears to favor those in the same group.

While most students can find at least one teacher to "buddy up" with, some students have the opposite problem and are seen as teachers' pets. Very smart students or very sweet and well-behaved kids are often singled out by teachers, much to the dismay of these students, who just want to fit in with their friends. The other kids will make fun of the teacher's pet, ostracizing him or her, adding to the pressure. If the child is a serious student and intentionally gets close to the teacher to obtain more help, and then is ridiculed for doing so, the situation is exacerbated.

School Stress #5: Stressed-Out Educators

Children take their cues from the adults around them. We all know how they imitate us, clomping around in our shoes, making the same gestures, and speaking with the same intonations as we do. We are aware of our obligations as role models and thus take special care to "behave" around our children, not swearing in their presence, refraining from smoking or drinking, using complete sentences, using correct grammar, and so on.

While parents are the most important role models for children, teachers are the second most influential. The modeling of educators greatly affects those children who are in the classroom six to eight hours a day (in some cases, an educator may see a child more than the parent does). When the teacher herself is stressed and anxious, some of that anxiety can trickle down to the children. Children are very alert and can sense when the teacher is under pressure, frazzled, stressed out. And today's teachers are among the most stressed.

According to a recent *Time* magazine report, people who deal with children are paid less, respected less, and regulated less than other professionals. (Interestingly, this is so even among doctors: Pediatricians' income ranks near the bottom of the physicians' scale.) In Michigan, preschool teachers with five years' experience earn $12,000; prison guards with the same seniority earn two-and-a-half times that, $30,000. Along with being underpaid, teachers are overworked, beleaguered with crowded classrooms and unmanageable work loads, and may suffer inadequate leadership, such as a principal who is inept. Added to this is the fact that children bring to school the problems they experience in their homes. Often educators find it impossible to provide all the emotional comfort and support needed for students to leave behind the pains they are feeling so that they can move into the role of learners. All of these factors conspire to produce teachers who suffer from stress and burnout regularly. Some of that stress translates into short temper and irritability in the classroom. Every symptom of stress the teacher feels is magnified in her students.

What You Can Do to Identify and
Alleviate School Stress

If your children find going to school really stressful, you are probably aware of that fact. What can you do to prevent or deal with such stress? The first step is awareness. Listen to your children when they talk about school. Ask questions about their teachers, about their tests, about the other students. Learn as much as you can about each situation that causes your children stress. Sometimes you won't be able to change the situation—for example, if the school is in a bad neighborhood. However, consider your options. If you can't make the neighborhood safer, do your best to change neighborhoods. Here are some other things you can do.

1. Inspect the school. This sounds amazingly simple, but you'd be surprised at how few parents go to their children's schools regularly. Perhaps you went to the school when you first moved into the neighborhood, or when your oldest child began attending there. How long ago was that? Schools change constantly. Even if you go to the school once or twice a year, that may not be enough. If you attend a special parents' night or go to a PTA meeting, you have seen very little of the real world of school. You may not have a realistic picture. Drop in unexpectedly. Go in the middle of the week, not on a Monday or a Friday. Go a few days after a holiday, when classes are just beginning to get back into their normal routine.

What should you look for at the school? Make a checklist. Look at the general cleanliness of the school. Does the trash in the halls seem to have been there a while, or was it just dropped at the last class break? Are the grounds maintained? Are graffiti present? Can you see signs that previous graffiti have been erased or painted over, or do the graffiti look as if they have been there for a long time? The general cleanliness of the school is a good indicator of the pride the school takes in itself. Of course, some schools have budget problems that have necessitated their making fewer repairs and laying off some staff. Be understanding if things are not as spic and span as you would like them to be. However, your child should not have to spend all day in a substandard environment.

2. Talk with the teachers and principal. Your children may groan when you tell them you are going to do this, but doing so is an integral step in getting a realistic picture of how much pressure is on your children. Does the teacher assign a lot of homework? Does he or she give the children as much individual attention as possible? Is she qualified to teach the subject, or is she learning it as she goes along? (Due to budget crises, some French teachers suddenly find themselves teaching Spanish.)

Ask the teacher what she thinks about your children's stress levels. Ask her to be honest with you and to cover not just the academic side of schooling but the personal one as well. She observes how your children fit in, whether they are part of the crowd, what the latest is in the broken heart department. She will probably be able to give you insights that your children (who tend to say, "nothin' " when you ask what happened at school today) cannot.

Talk to the principal about crime in the school and what is being done to lessen it. Again, every school is different; some schools have to deal with being in terrible neighborhoods, and some don't have the money to hire guards. But every principal should have a plan that he or she is willing to share with you. If you know the steps that are being taken to lessen the impact of crime, you can tell your children and let them know not only that you care but that someone else is looking out for them.

3. Prepare your children for the job of education. Try to integrate school and home. Give your children a quiet place to study, away from the other siblings, the television, the noise of the neighborhood. Set aside a special place that is theirs alone. Agree on a regular time for studying, postponing other activities until after homework time.

"What helped me most," said Alex, "was how my parents helped me to get organized. My father designed a bookcase and got me a desk that had a lot of drawers for my papers and stuff. My mom set up a file and showed me how to use it, and put a huge wall calendar in front of me. I could see my assignments at a glance, especially the long-term ones like papers that I usually put off until the last minute. Every time I sat down at my desk I felt like I was ready to go to work, and I started using my time better. I didn't have to run around every night getting things together, because they were all in one spot and no one else was allowed to mess with them."

4. Stay involved: Show an active interest. When children are very young and school is one big adventure to them, they can't wait to get home to tell you everything that happened that day. As children get older, they talk more and more to their friends and less to you about the minutiae of school. It is therefore up to you to maintain an active interest. Don't take "Fine, I guess" as an answer when you ask how school is going. Naturally, there is a line between being nosy and being interested (as far as the average teenager is concerned, if you so much as look inquisitively at him, you're being nosy), but even if getting information about school is like pulling teeth, don't give up. You are sending your children the message that you care about how they are doing.

Help your children with their homework, but do so judiciously. You don't have to do the homework yourself, nor should you get into big arguments with an uncooperative or uncomprehending child. Helping with homework can be as simple as knowing what chapter is being covered in your daughter's biology class and encouraging her to talk about it. For your third-grader, you can bring home flash cards with the multiplication tables and work on them at the dinner table. Don't plead lack of time as a reason not to get involved. It takes only a few minutes to discuss an assignment.

5. Send them off with a good night's sleep, breakfast, and a smile. All children need eight to ten hours of sleep in order to feel refreshed the next day. Some children need even more. Remember, in addition to going to school and managing a work load, your child is growing and developing. Sleep is important. If your child is sixteen or younger, monitor his or her bedtime hour. That means lights, radio, and stereo off.

We all know that breakfast, the first meal, is the most important meal of the day, and how your children begin their day depends a lot on you. What are those first few minutes like at your breakfast table? Do you greet your children with a smile and tell them it's going to be a great day? Do you know enough about their school days to remember when the science project is due and whether there is a Spanish test that afternoon? It's very comforting to children to know that you are there in spirit, that you're staying involved and rooting for them.

The food you put on the table can help reduce stress as well. See to it that nutritious foods are served. It can be as simple as a shake made of yogurt and a banana, or bran cereal, or whatever your children like that provides energy for them. If you can possibly have the food all ready and sitting at their place at the table, you can prevent those small arguments over the frosted donuts and leftover pizza.

And speaking of arguments, early morning is no time for them. You know how stressful it can be to begin the day by yelling at your children for something they did or didn't do; imagine how stressful it is for them to be yelled at! Many morning problems are caused by a lack of time. People who feel rushed are more irritable and more likely to snap at others. Getting up just fifteen minutes earlier will allow you to get a grip on yourself and feel more comfortable, spilling those good feelings over onto your children.

Finally, don't forget the pep talk! Talk to your children before they leave. Tell them how well they are doing in school, and how you are certain they will do a great job on today's quiz or test or project. Remind them how good they felt about past successes. Everyone enjoys reliving past triumphs. A motivating speech can get your children revved up for what is coming their way. And even if you get a bit carried away and your dramatic "Win one for the Gipper" speech leaves your kids laughing at you, so what? A good laugh—sometimes called an "internal message"—is a great way to reduce stress and begin the day.

6. Education is lifelong: Set a good example. Children do as their parents *do*, not always as they say. If you get excited about books and new ideas, your children will, too. If you act as if anything worth doing is worth doing well, your children will feel the same. You can sign up for adult education classes through community colleges or take career enrichment courses at work. Involve your children in your own education. Show them your books and papers—even the ones on which you *didn't* get an A! Tell them what you are doing in class, what you are learning. If you can't attend a class, tell your children about your own education in the Good Old Days, and how much that education helped you.

Casey's mother used to be very self-conscious about her lack of education. Even though she had a good job, she had dropped out of high school to marry and start a family. When her children were eleven and thirteen, she began studying for a high school equivalency certificate, and eventually she earned one. She then got so busy at work she was unable to begin taking community college classes as she had hoped. Her children, she worried, would get the message that she was quitting. She talked it over with a friend and got the idea to go to the library for a self-taught course in Spanish. She brought home cassette tapes and printed materials, set aside a half hour for Spanish study five nights a week, and let nothing interfere with it. She talked a lot about how much she enjoyed learning something new . . . and soon her children were trying to get her to speak Spanish to them so they could learn, too. The highlight came when she heard Casey talking on the phone to her best friend and saying, "Yeah, my mom is a perpetual student. She's always studying something. I hope I can stay that motivated when I'm old." Although a bit disappointed to be called old at thirty-four, Casey's mother felt satisfied. Her daughter was proud of her and got the idea that education was a good thing.

Gauging School Stress: A Checklist for Parents

No two children are alike. Within your own family, you are probably amazed at how different your kids are. No two children react exactly the same way to stress in school. It's important for you to be aware of your children's feelings about school, feelings that may take a little digging to get out. There's no need to cross-examine your children every day; however, a few questions every now and then can keep you up to date. The following checklist is a start.

School Stress Checklist

- Do your children often say that they dislike going to school?

- Do your children like and admire their teachers? Do your children believe their teachers like and admire them? Do they think the teachers are fair?

- Do your children dawdle in the morning, postponing leaving as long as possible?

- Do your children refuse to set out their clothing and books the night before, preferring not to think about the next day at school until they absolutely have to?

- Do your children talk about their friends at school, or do they seem to have no stories of what they and their buddies did?

- Do your children mention that other students treat them in a negative manner, mocking them or threatening them?

- Do most of your children's comments focus on their academic failures and fears ("I flunked last week's test, and I'll probably flunk this one too")?

- Do your children seem afraid of the school environment itself, worried about dangers on the school grounds or about the other kids?

- Do your children seem not to care how they dress for school, putting more effort into looking good after school for the kids in the neighborhood than for their friends at school?

Over the years you will develop your own checklist as you become aware of your child's strengths and weaknesses. The goal here is to recognize the warning signs that alert you to stress caused by your child's schooling. While occasional stress is natural—and can even be beneficial to some children who need pressure to get things done—the careful parent keeps a watchful eye out for overload.

Learning at Home

Families are the single most important influence on children's lives. According to Gordon Dryden and Jeanette Vos, most brain researchers are convinced that 50 percent of a person's ability to learn is developed in the first four years of life. This means that home, not school, is the most important educational institution in the land.

More and more parents are finding that they want a structured teaching program for their preschoolers at home. The state of Missouri has developed a program called PAT: Parents as Teachers. More than 100,000 families with children under three have been involved in PAT. Every month the parents are visited by an educator who gives information on the next phase of the child's development and offers ways parents can help the child through the phase, including tips on constructive play, effective discipline, and home safety. The educator brings along toys and books suitable for the child and leaves a list of suggestions to help stimulate the child's interest in learning.

Supporters of the PAT program say it is more consistently successful than Head Start or similar programs, because it gets to the children early, when they are still most receptive. In addition, it helps the parents get involved. With a program like Head Start, children have to return home to the same disadvantaged environment, to parents who were not a part of the child's learning day. In addition, the cost per child is relatively low with PAT, approximately $250 per year. Given the twelve million youngsters in America under age three in any given year, the program would cost three billion dollars a year, an amount that may be the best investment in national security and productivity our nation could make.

Another home-based parent education program that has shown success is HIPPY: Home Instruction Program for Preschool Youngsters. Started in Israel in 1969, it now operates in more than twenty other countries. HIPPY trains parents of children aged four to six directly in their own homes. The parents are taught proper nutrition, effective discipline, how to assist with homework—any skill to help them better care for their children. Parents are visited every two weeks and meet with other parents twice a month. Like PAT, the results of this in-home instruction have been excellent. This program has been given a big boost in America through success in Arkansas, where literacy has increased due to the program.

Parents who are involved in their children's education early on send the message to their children that education is important, and they themselves are more likely to remain closely involved with this education throughout their child's school career. Just as we adults need encouragement and support in our work, children—of all ages—do, too. It all begins with the family, in the homeplace.

PART IV

Family Stress

Chapter 7

HOW THE FAMILY
CREATES STRESS
FOR CHILDREN

S ome years back I was lamenting about my particularly cum-
bersome schedule to my good friend Joe Batten, a management consultant and author. Joe provided a piece of advice that
has been helpful over the years. "No matter what age or stage,"
he said, "all of life is a juggling and balancing act. Just remember
that there are glass balls and rubber balls in life. The goal is to
know which is which. Family, health, and friends are the glass
balls. *You must never drop the glass balls.*" It's good advice. A
family life that is rich and nourishing is a powerful source of joy
and satisfaction, fun and warmth, strength and reassurance; it
can sustain us through times when other facets of life are turbulent. The bonds created between family members are among the
most durable anchors in life.

Just as a family can provide nourishment and support or serve as a buffer against outside forces, it can also be a source of stress and pain for family members. Just as a family can create a strong foundation on which a child can confidently build her life, a family can also be a desert of shifting sands, creating duress and dysfunction for the child.

Julianne

Julianne liked to be called juli. "When you write this," she said to me, "please spell my name the way I like it. Not with a capital J, not with a y or an ie at the end, just an i." Her brand of soft-spoken assertiveness had a style and charm of its own. Entering the fourth month of her seventeenth year, juli had poise and an air of calmness that belied the enormity of the stress in her life.

As is the case with too many children, much of juli's stress was induced by her parents, stepparents, and parents' lovers, several of whom were muddling through their own less-than-ideal lives. Born prematurely, largely due to the brutal beating inflicted on her then-sixteen-year-old mother by her sailor husband, juli was not to escape her father's rage and abuse either. He sexually assaulted her for the first time when she was three. Punishments were unusually harsh and cruel. Wetting the bed always brought a spanking; sometimes juli would huddle in a corner of the bathroom thinking that if she could remain awake she wouldn't wet the bed. When her father found her out of bed, that too brought on his rage. Bad dreams and nightmares followed; her crying and screams from the fright she felt brought scolding by her mother, who feared juli would wake her father. Sometimes juli's mother would slap her to make her be quiet. For juli, nurturing and soothing were hard to come by.

Eventually juli's father left her mother. In some ways, it was good. The sexual assaults decreased to twice a month—when her father had visitation rights. In other ways, it was not such a relief. Her mother started a cycle of heavy drinking and frequent dating. Juliane was left in the care of numerous babysitters. It was a time of loneliness and family chaos.

At eight, juli went to stay with her grandparents some two hundred miles away. There she encountered for the first time a normal child's life, complete with paternal and maternal affection. When her grandmother died a year later, juli returned home to her mother.

Her mother married for the second time when juli was eleven. Ben, an officer in the navy, was terrific. He helped juli with homework, he talked rather then yelled, and conversations at the dinner table became common. Ben helped her to join a girls' softball team and bought juli her first baseball glove. When he encouraged her to join the school team and helped her improve her skills at batting, he won her heart. One "dark day," as juli called it, her beloved stepfather arrived home to find his wife in bed with another man. Divorce followed. When Ben remarried several years later, juli lost touch with him; she misses him dearly.

Junior high brought its own perils, but juli liked school and did well there, earning respect from both her teachers and her classmates. It was her escape into a world with order, a respite from chaos. School achievement and success helped juli see herself as a capable and competent person, contributing to a more positive sense of self—at least while at school.

Now—at the tender age of seventeen—juli has had two abortions, dropped out to pay for the last one, and has just returned to an alternative school to complete her high school education. Amazingly, she is open about her life and exceptionally optimistic about her future. Counted among her "successes" is the final break from her father; the last sexual encounter was nearly three years ago, and she refuses to see him now, no longer mandated to do so by the courts. She is finding a way to come to terms with her mother's limitations without relinquishing their relationship and without becoming a codependent to her mother's personality disorders. Juli is thinking hard about what she wants to do with her life and about ways she can shape her life in a productive and meaningful way, rather than "stumbling through it like other adults I know."

Though we don't know yet how juli will fare as she encounters new challenges and obstacles in her life, there are some indications that she may be successful in moving beyond what was a most unfair beginning. She still has faith that others will encourage her and assist her when she needs help (no doubt a contribution from Ben). When she discovered that the local Jaycees were planning to sponsor three local youths for a six-week summer session abroad, for example, she wasted no time in getting an application and asking her school counselor and several teachers to help her put together a competitive portfolio. Their assistance enabled her to become a finalist. That summer she left for England.

Family Chaos, Childhood Stress

Juli's story is dramatic, but unfortunately it is not uncommon. Her family is just one example of the thousands of families that in their own ways create stress in children. A chaotic homeplace breeds stress. Parents who are physically abusive or emotionally distant create pain for their children. For better or for worse, all behavior has an effect on our children. Effective parents contribute to a child's becoming healthy and functional. The effects of dysfunctional parents can generally be seen in their troubled children, who in turn pass dysfunction along to *their* children. Parents are a child's first teachers; what the children see is what they "know." Home is a child's training ground for learning how people treat others.

The health of a family unit, and of each family member as well, depends on how the adults—individually and then as a couple—respond to the duties and responsibilities of being conscientious parents. The principles of keeping a family healthy and functional are fairly straightforward:

- parents are aware of the importance of their actions;
- parents are aware of the causes of their actions and the effects on their children;
- parents set challenging yet fair and attainable expectations for each child, to develop individual strengths and talents;
- parents effectively guide and discipline their children;
- parents apply consequences in ways that help children learn boundaries without emotionally or physically hurting their children in the process.

In short, the most powerful factor in preventing and/or causing stress in children is the home environment. The well-being of children is threatened when external havoc (such as a parent going through a divorce) becomes internal (one or both are emotionally debilitated to the point where children are used as scapegoats for the parents' fears and frustrations), first for the parents and then for their children.

There Is No "Typical" Family Anymore

The circumstances that surround the lives of today's families are different from those of a decade ago. The Norman Rockwell image—a father working outside the home, a housewife mother, nearby grandparents who are all to happy to help out, and a few kids running around with skinned knees, getting a lot of hugs—is just that, an image (and one that rarely ever actually existed). The "family" has changed. Of the more than ninety-eight million American households, almost twenty-three million consist of one adult and one child. Today, nearly 74 percent of women are in the workforce, and many of these are the head of their household. According to the 1990 census, of every one hundred children born today:

- seventeen will be born out of wedlock;
- forty-eight will have parents who divorce before the children are eighteen;
- sixteen will have parents who separate;
- six will have at least one parent die before the children are eighteen.

That means that of every one hundred children, only thirteen will become adults in "normal" families.

Childhood, defined by stages of intense physical and emotional growth, renders every day a new experience in uncharted waters. As a child progresses through the various developmental stages of infancy, childhood, adolescence, and young adulthood, a number of behavioral and emotional changes result in varying degrees of stress. While going through his own traumatic stages of growth, the child needs assurance and support from his parents. Yet children today are likely to confront the stress, strains, and pressures of today's times with less parental support than did yesterday's child, and with few other adults who serve as anchors.

Our mothers had time for us—we were the focus of their lives. Many of us had mothers who made full-time careers of child rearing, who were revered by society for staying home and taking care of us. Motherhood was a full-time job. Today it is a part-time position, its status falling somewhere between a mother's gainful employment and her body's tone and fitness. Many women cannot stay at home and rear their children full-time, but rather juggle careers and families. There aren't enough hours in the day; something has to give. Too often what gives is the amount of time and support a young person receives. During the most vulnerable and impressionable time of life, a child must cope with stress, strains, and pressures of life nearly alone. In its report on the wellness of children, the 1991 National Commission on Children stated, "Children at every income level lack time, attention, and guidance from parents and other caring adults."

Separation and Divorce

In the 1950s divorce was relatively uncommon. By 1965 one in every three marriages was destined for divorce, and by 1980 one in two marriages ended in divorce, as has been true of the nineties. The rate of increase in family breakup was alarming in the sixties and seventies, but families took comfort in the conviction that after a time of grieving, children of divorce would bounce back, with relatively little damage. Unfortunately, that has not been the case. In her book *Second Chances: Men, Women, & Children a Decade after Divorce*, a ten-year study of divorced families, psychologist Judith Wallerstein confirmed that the pain of divorce is not transient for children, that the trauma haunts them into adulthood. Not only did divorce create for them a struggle to escape a lingering shadow that darkened their own search for love, but it was "the single most important cause of enduring pain and anomie in their lives." Even more troubling, Wallerstein found that the dislocation visited upon children by their parents' divorce, far from disappearing after adolescence, turned out to be permanent. She found that among the most devastating effects of divorce for girls was that it "seriously derailed" them between the ages of nineteen and twenty-three, and that feelings of hurt and pain stemming from the divorce would "plague them forever." Divorce had detrimental effects on male children as well. Wallerstein found a lack of direction and a "sense of having little control over their lives" were common results of divorce for boys, and that the experience of divorce could "permanently cripple them emotionally." Clearly, divorce affects the emotional lives of children, with aftershocks reaching well into their adult lives.

It is unlikely that such grim findings will reverse a decision to divorce. And for children, being brought up in a dysfunctional family can be much worse than being brought up in a divorced family. Because their parents' divorce is so painful for children, and because the repercussions of divorce can cause such long-term damage for children, parents need to be especially attentive about explaining to their children what divorce will mean for the children. They must reassure them that the parents are doing it to make things *better* and will help the children through it. It is especially important to reassure children that the divorce is not their fault. Divorce is a family crisis, and families must deal with it as one. Parents must tell children where Daddy is going to live and where Mommy is going to live and that they are going to try to make the new homes as comfortable as possible. At the same time, they must be honest and say that it is going to cause upset for a while. Above all, parents must give the children permission to love both parents and must never allow them to be made a part of the problems that plague their parents.

Single-Parent Families

Living with one parent who is happy and emotionally healthy is a better experience than living in a home where two adults are unhappy with each other. Perhaps what is most stressful for the single-parent family is that often the parent is carrying a greater number of responsibilities. Family life becomes hectic, a battle for survival. Tasks that were once taken for granted, such as shopping, cooking, and cleaning, can become major challenges. Little luxuries, like membership in a health club or dinners at nice restaurants, might no longer be possible due to economic hardships. The need to make a living can take precedence over the traditional family roles of nurturing and comforting.

Would You Rather Have One, Two, Three, or Four (or More) Parents?

Having four parents (rather than two) can make life complicated. Children today have a significant likelihood of having stepparents; they may find themselves with a father, stepfather, mother, stepmother, and four sets of grandparents, all of whom have very definite ideas about child rearing. A child's loyalties are naturally torn. And unfortunately, by the time a child is eighteen, she might have had two or even three stepparents, all of whom she has been told to love and respect. Imagine the difficulty a child has becoming close to and trusting a stepparent when she sees that the stepparent might not be around that long anyway. Children often wonder where they fit in, how important they are, not only to their own biological parent but to this new stepparent who has suddenly taken over.

Absentee Parents

Even children who live with both of their biological parents may have "absentee" parents in a figurative sense—parents who are not with their children enough to give them the time and nurturing the children need. In many cases, both parents work, out of necessity or desire. According to the U.S. Department of Labor, more than thirty-eight million American children have moms who are employed outside the home. That's 62 percent of all children under eighteen. Since 1950, the number of women who combine career and family roles has steadily increased. Parents who juggle both family and occupational roles are often in conflict, conflict that produces stress in both the parents and the children.

The statistics bear out the fact that working parents don't get to spend as much time with their children as both they and the children would like. A study by the University of Michigan Institute for Social Research found that mothers who work outside the home spend only eleven minutes each weekday and thirty minutes each weekend day playing exclusively with their children, a period defined as "quality time." Fathers spend even less, averaging only eight minute per weekday and fourteen minutes on the weekends. Parents feel guilty about the lack of time they spend with their children; children feel abandoned and unwanted.

Sibling Separation and Addition

In some divorces, the children are not all taken by the same parent. This means that in addition to losing a parent, the child loses a brother or a sister, perhaps the only other person who understands how painful the divorce is. Even worse is a child's having to cope with a new set of siblings, total strangers who share his house and sometimes even his room. A child who has been alone with his parent for a while might greatly resent having to share that parent with other children, especially if they are very young and demand a lot of attention. Or he might be afraid to become close to the siblings, fearful that they will be taken away with the next divorce.

The Handicapped Family Member

Not all problems within the family stem from divorce or remarriage. There are many intact families that have their own stresses. A sibling might be physically handicapped or mentally retarded. Children in this situation often feel very strongly that their parents give more time and attention to the handicapped child than to them. The healthy child, furthermore, has to deal with the taunts others give her sibling, and she either fights on behalf of her sibling or feels guilty for not stepping in. She often has a physical burden put on her, too: "You look after your sister, Jean. She depends on you to get her to school safely." That type of responsibility is a great stressor for a child of any age. There is also the guilt of being normal and healthy while the other child is not. If a healthy sibling contracts a disease or meets with an accident, the other children naturally worry whether they could be next.

"Weird" siblings can cause nearly as much stress as handicapped brothers and sisters. If a shy child in a very conservative neighborhood has a sister who shaves half her head and wears navy blue lipstick, the more reserved child is embarrassed by it. As LaDonna put it, "My friend's sister is in a wheelchair and drools, and that's not cool, but she can't help it. My sister shaves her head and wears a ring in her nose by choice. She's such a geek it's embarrassing to be around her."

Abuse

The child who is physically hurt by acts of unfair discipline or by acts of sexual abuse by parents, stepparents, or relatives faces pain so deadly that it takes a lifetime to sort out. To be hurt in such ways is simply devastating. Any abuse impairs a child's ability to construct a healthy self-identity and makes caring about others difficult.

Parental Baggage

Children in a nonabusive suburban family with a minivan, two dogs, and all family members present and accounted for are not always free of stress. The stereotype of the stage mother who pushes her daughter to become the Broadway star she never was is mirrored in the suburban parents who push their children to get the grades necessary to enter the Ivy League colleges they never attended. Parents can subconsciously use their children to fulfill their own fantasies.

Unfortunately, it's all too easy for a parent to harbor feelings of discontent over things they haven't accomplished, goals they haven't met. Some parents started families early and as a result had to forgo college or forfeit career opportunities. These parents love their children. Still, they may think of what they could have done or would be doing if it were not for the children. The large checks for braces, the expenses involved in providing for children with special needs, or the continual pressure to save for college can cause parents to wonder just how much sacrifice they should make. Even the most loving, giving, nurturing parents can unwittingly transmit these longings and resentments to their children. Children at any age have sensitive antennae and are quick to internalize problems, thinking that everything is their fault.

Poverty

One of the primary sources of stress in children is poverty. According to an article in *U.S. News & World Report*, seven million white children and four million black children under age fifteen in the U.S. live below the poverty line. Children are nearly twice as likely to be poor as adults, with one out of five children suffering from poverty. Children suffer direct stress from poverty, wondering why they can't have new clothes for school or a big birthday cake like their friends. They also suffer indirect stress from poverty: the abuse that their stressed parents inflict on them. The children of the poor are seven to eight times more likely to be neglected or abused. Studies show that children tend to treat their own children as they were treated, perpetuating patterns of stress-induced child abuse. Today's stressed children are time bombs waiting to explode, to inflict violence on future generations.

Identifying Family Stress: A Checklist

No family is without stress. And every family member will differ in terms of what he finds stressful. The goal is to identify what creates stress for your child and to understand how it affects him or her. The following checklist can help you determine just how much family-induced stress has been placed upon your child.

Family Stress Checklist

1. Has there been a divorce in your family since your child's birth?

2. Has there been more than one divorce since your child's birth?

3. Has your child lived alone with you, without another parent?

4. Have you had a full-time job that required you to put your child into day care?

5. Has your child had to live under the same roof as a stepparent?

6. Has your child had more than one stepparent?

7. Has your child had to live under the same roof as stepsiblings?

8. Has your child had to share a room with a stepsibling?

9. Has your child lost a parent to death?

10. Has your child had to adjust to the birth of a new child?

11. Have you moved, so that your child had to attend a new school and make new friends?

12. Is anyone in your family handicapped, physically or mentally?

13. Does anyone in your family have a drug or alcohol problem?

14. Does your family have financial difficulties?

15. Has anyone in your family been fired or laid off from work?

16. Has your child ever been sexually abused?

Be alert to things that can cause stress before they happen, so that you can prepare your children. For example, if there is going to be some financial belt-tightening due to a job change, talk it over with your children. Very young children, of course, won't understand everything, but they can be helped to understand that there will be some changes. As you know, most children thrive on routine and become very nervous when things are altered. Preparation is vital.

Just because you love to go bungee jumping does not mean your children will like to challenge themselves. In the comedy world, you can be sure that a brawny football player will have a bookworm son. Be alert to how you feel about stress so that you can increase your sensitivity to your children's. What might not faze you a bit could drive your children to distraction.

What Parents Can Do to Alleviate Family Stress

How do you develop a plan to reduce stress in the home? The key word is *support.* Research shows that children who are good copers tend to have parents who are warm, loving, and supportive. While respecting their children's independence, such parents hold firm to their convictions about what is right, explaining their reasons to the child while insisting on proper behavior. Combining strong support with challenge is the goal. Families that produce relatively well-adjusted children (alas, the Perfect Parent is still only a Hollywood creation) often open doors for children. They encourage them to grow until they are ready to move through those doors.

Parents who are skilled at making the home a relaxing, nurturing place to be, rather than a stress site, do the following:

1. Supervise. The most stress-free children are those with supervision. A common mistake that parents make is to think that children, especially teens, can fend for themselves. Supervision does not necessarily mean being home with fresh-baked cookies when Junior arrives from school. The realities of the working world mean that many parents can't spend as much time with their children in person that they would like. Arranging for child care and encouraging after-school activities are good ways to make sure children are physically supervised.

2. Establish and enforce clear boundaries. Children are always testing us, searching for the next-to-last straw they can pile on the camel's back. They want to know just how far we will let them go, how far our love can be pushed. Busy parents unfortunately seem to let discipline be one of the first casualties of their harried lives. They spend so little time with their children that they want those few hours to be fun rather than filled with discipline, rules, and punishment. As Mrs. DeVincenzi says, "I see my son only during dinner time. Then he goes off to softball practice and to the library to study or to hang out with his friends, and I often go back to the office to get in a little overtime. The last thing I want to do is spend dinner yelling at him about breaking his curfew or having an occasional beer. How important are those things, really?" In and of themselves, the actions may not be important, but the symbolism behind them is. Children need structure in their lives. If you set rules and boundaries for your children but then do not implement consequences for breaking those rules, you send a message either that the rules for good behavior are not especially important, or that you are not serious about enforcing them.

When you discipline, be sure to discipline fairly. If you (or your spouse) need to learn better ways to get your children to behave, turn to your local school and call the principal, nurse, or school counselor to ask for recommendations. Get help. Doing so is not a sign of weakness but a healthy sign of caring. When you feel more comfortable dealing with your children, they sense it and become more comfortable dealing with themselves. In addition, by teaching them proper behavior now, you prevent them from having the stresses that come with being socially unacceptable later.

3. Spend time together. Parents who feel guilty about the effects of their busy lives on their children often shower their kids with material gifts. Children of divorced parents often become pros at getting goodies from both sides. But deep down we know that it's time with parents, not presents, that helps our children. Not all children need the same amount of time with their parents; there are some age groups whose fondest wish is to spend as little time with their parents as possible! But even the busiest parents must take time to spend exclusively with their children, making them feel that they are important.

4. Learn how to be a family. Some parents come from dysfunctional families themselves and don't have any real sense of what a family should be. You may feel that you need outside help. Seek a support group. While a family may, in some special cases, need actual therapeutic help, it is very useful just to have the opportunity to vent feelings with other families in discussion or therapy groups. You will find a number of local organizations that offer counseling and support for parents or for families. Ask your school, church, temple, or YMCA to suggest some.

5. Talk it over. Communication is the real key in reducing family stress. Put your best communication skills forward. People must feel safe—that they will be earnestly listened to and not judged—before they will talk about their innermost feelings, especially the uncomfortable ones. Parents must be willing to talk to each other in private in order to arrive at an agreement on troublesome issues. For example, one child may dislike it when her stepfather always introduces her as his daughter. "Mom, he is *not* my father, and I don't want him telling others that he is. I have a dad. I want him to call me *Susan*." Her mother needs to talk to the stepfather and tell him of the child's feelings. They must arrive at an understanding of why Susan feels as she does, and everyone should be reassured of the respect and caring that the others have for them.

Parents also need to agree on discipline and matters of upbringing in order to present a cohesive front to their children. Children, especially small ones, become very anxious when their parents fight or bicker. Good communication skills can prevent parents from sending confusing double signals. Blended families, in particular, need to develop good interpersonal skills. The Stepfamily Association of America (listed in the resource section of this book) offers counseling referrals, support groups, and educational publications containing advice on legal, financial, and practical ways of lowering the stress of stepparenting.

6. Encourage your child to invite friends home. Make it easy for your child to bring friends home by being openminded, friendly, and slow to criticize those friends. If you shut out your child's friends you also cut off an important part of his world. His response will be to separate his home life from his social life, and this will alienate you from the latter. A child's home is an important sanctuary. Adolescents will flock to the homes where parents are open and accessible.

7. Have family fun. Don't forget to have fun. Children as well as adults need to be joyous. Do you know how to *play* with your children? Helping them to have fun, to live with zest and zeal, maximizes self-fulfillment and minimizes stress and burnout. Foster in your children the enjoyment of the love and support of family and friends, the joy possible through spiritual awareness, the sheer exuberance that new challenges can bring. Too often we are so wrapped up in educating our children that we forget to "teach" through example how to have fun.

Go outdoors and play games with your children. Try to develop an interest in sports with them. Travel if you can, even if your finances allow you only to go on camping trips in the next county. Be spectators together at fun events, from Ninja Turtles karate demonstrations to fashion shows. Have tea parties with your children and their imaginary friends. Do whatever it takes to bring about that most wonderful of sounds, your children's laughter.

Very few of us truly outgrow our emotional dependence on our families, even when we begin new families of our own. This dependence can magnify any stresses inherent in family situations. These stresses can be inevitable and out of the child's control (such as divorce and remarriage, death, or financial hardships), or they can be somewhat within the child's control (such as behavior problems and discipline). It is important for parents to identify the sources of stress, to assess them realistically (not worrying that admitting their families are less than perfect will somehow make them parenting failures), and to take steps to cope with such stresses. Many stresses will never be completely eliminated, but there are always things that can be done to mitigate their effects on children. Learn about the stresses, and learn to work through them to help make the family a place of security, solace, and love.

Chapter 8

WHAT ABOUT MY STRESS?

W hen I conduct workshops for parents on the stress and strains of children, someone will invariably exclaim, only half-jokingly, "Children's stress! What about mine? I'm the one under stress!" When the amusement subsides, parents then ask questions pertaining to their own stress levels and the effects of passing that stress along to their children: "How can I help my child if *I'm* under stress?" "How much damage do I cause my children if I don't yet have it under control, if they see me struggle to manage my response to stress?" "What if my spouse or ex has conflicting values about how we are raising our children?" Next come questions asked in a very serious vein, those that reveal the parents' recognition of their greatest concern—the awesome task of raising a child. "How can I be sure I'm doing

the right things for my child?" "How can I help my child become a healthy, capable, and loving human being?"

Over the years in my work, I have found these to be common
concerns of many parents—parents of newborns, parents of
teenagers, parents who watch with hopeful eyes as their adult
children go about parenting their own children. Unfortunately,
children don't come with a parts and maintenance manual, as do
our automobiles, nor with directions for assembly and care, as
do some of our children's toys. Pondering whether or not we are
doing (or have done) the right things for our children is at the
heart of much of the joy, the pain, and the stress of parenting.

It can be comforting as well as helpful to recognize that you
are not alone in your parenting concerns, spoken or unspoken.
It can be useful to know how to quiet the sometimes insecure
voice inside your head. It's important to understand that being
a parent doesn't mean you always have the answers. It's okay to
ask for help sometimes. This chapter is designed to identify and
articulate some of the stresses parents experience in the many
hats they wear as they raise their kids.

There are few jobs as important or as difficult as parenting.
Parents constantly wonder if they are doing a good enough job
in raising their children. Concern about our children's physical,
mental, emotional, and spiritual welfare never goes away, not
even when our children leave home. My parents, now in their
seventies, still express concern for their six children, periodically
calling to hear how we are, still pondering the effects of their
parenting on us.

Am I a Good Parent?

The mere fact of being a parent raises a lot of questions. Of the many experiences in our life, rearing children can be the most intense, providing not only fervent joy but occasionally grave sadness. Our children cling to and reject us, adore and barely tolerate us. What we learn from these impassioned experiences leaves an indelible mark—on both parent and child.

Parenting teaches some of the most profound lessons in our lives. It helps us satisfy the unfinished business of our own unmet childhood needs—such as the need for more hugging, kissing, and cuddling as children—or to recreate the feelings of closeness, caring, and benevolence we received from our parents. The love, kindness, fairness, neglect, rage, and hurt of our own childhoods pour out into our relationships with our children. In meeting the needs of these dependent people we cherish so much, our actions are often derived from the love and acceptance that we feel we ourselves deserve. Our parenting actions can be a reflection of our own self-esteem. *Nurturing children often is an exercise in perfecting our own natures.*

Parenthood creates a major shift in focus, motivating us to move beyond our own self-centered concerns and to care deeply about the needs of another. It can help us focus more clearly on the meaning of our own personal journey through time and keep us from sleepwalking through life. Parenting can complete our own experience of childhood, after our feelings of aloneness, and awaken within us deep-seated experiences from our past, forcing us to reconcile or make peace with them. The need to give priority to that which gives meaning can cause us to live more fully than we might otherwise. Children forever alter our consciousness.

In the process of helping our children grow and develop skills to surmount life's challenges, we discover much about ourselves. Teaching our children how to pass the test of life presents parents with an opportunity to learn as well. Sometimes we discover that we don't have the answer key we wish we had, and the result is many questions:

- How good am I at having complete and full time responsibility for another human being?

- How can I know what each of my children needs? They are all so different.

- How can I rear my children to work toward purposeful goals, to succeed in ways that give their lives substance and joy and meaning?

- What type of life-style should I provide my children? Is it better to live in an upscale neighborhood, even if I have to scrimp in other areas to afford doing so? Should I move to a neighborhood that has the best schools, even if it is farther from my job or inconvenient in other ways?

- Should I move to be closer to the children's grandparents and other relatives, so that my children know their family and have the benefit of the family's love and emotional support?

- Should I insist my children get jobs as soon as they can to teach them the value of money, or should I support them and let them enjoy the carefree days of childhood as long as possible?

- Should I accept a new job that pays more money
  or is more fulfilling if it means my children have to
  move away from their friends and their schools?
  Will the extra money make their lives easier,
  or would the move be a selfish one on my part?

- Should I have another child? How will having or not
  having more siblings affect my children? Will they
  have more love from a big family, or will they get
  less attention?

Am I a Good Role Model?

All of us hope we are being good role models and sending
the right messages to our children. But we wonder constantly
whether we are doing the right thing. We learn—sometimes not
soon enough—that *doing things right* and *doing the right things*
are not the same, that they produce very different outcomes in
our children. We need to ask *what* should I be doing—what
things are more important than others? Questions such as the
following are steady reminders that our children can push our
emotional buttons:

- What makes me act the way I do at times? Am I
  capable of controlling my stress and frustrations rather
  than taking them out on my children? I want to
  love and praise them, but sometimes I can't hold
  back the negative expression of my fears. How can
  I always be in control of my actions and be a model
  parent? What should I tell my child when I have
  erred?

- Am I more likely to yell at than to talk with my child? Am I willing to take the time to explain how to do something over and over and over, or am I more likely just to give up and do it myself?

- Do I call my child by a demeaning nickname, such as Goofy or Klutzy or Buttface? What should I do when I get out of control and say negative things or swear at my children?

- Do I give flip responses when my child tells me of a problem, saying things like, "I'm not surprised" or "Not again!" or "You probably deserved it"?

- Do I ridicule my children to get rid of my own frustrations?

- Am I teaching the values I want to impart? Have I clearly identified for myself the values I have and wish to pass along to my children? If my children have already established values I think are wrong, how can I help them to change those values?

- How much love and respect do my children feel for me? Do I feel I am doing my best parenting possible?

- Am I letting my children get to know me as an individual, not just as a mom or dad? Do they feel they can be friends with me, that they like me as a person and not just fear me as an authority figure?

- Do my children feel they can come to me with their problems without fear of ridicule or dismissal? Do they respect my opinion enough to seek it out?

- Do my children feel proud of me? Do they respect the work I do? Do they think I am attractive or handsome? How do I get my children to respect me more?

- Do my children know that I respect them? Do I emphasize to them that they have the right to make their own choices, that I am here to help them, not to force my own choices on them?

- Do my children feel that I am involved in their daily lives? Do I know the names of their teachers, bus drivers, best friends, rivals, favorite television shows? Do I remember to ask about important events, like how the oral report went or what Brenda said to Kelly last night?

- Do I help my children become stronger physically, with good nutrition at home and suggestions for eating well away from home? Do I help them with an informal exercise program or involve them in sports?

- Have I taught my children to respect their bodies, not to abuse them with drugs and alcohol? Am I setting a good example by doing the same? If I use drugs or alcohol, am I explaining the difference between my doing so and a child's doing so in language my child can understand and respect?

- Do I help my children become stronger emotionally? Do I build their self-esteem with praise and affirmation?

- Do I help my children develop spiritually? Do I
  discuss my spirituality with them and let them
  know what it means to me?

Family Frustrations

Jim, a father of four, said to me in a recent workshop, "I got divorced four years ago and gained custody of my children. It was hard trying to conduct my career while raising these children, and I thought they were a liability to my work. I can hardly believe that thought crossed my mind, because I now think of my children not only as the greatest asset I have, but also as my portfolio."

A family is the greatest source of joy, and it can be the greatest source of stress, as well. How can we make sure our children get the most love and the least stress as possible from their families? Wanting to make the family unit a healthy one, and to create a nourishing and enjoyable experience of being together as a family, causes parents to ask themselves these questions:

- Am I presenting the other parent in a positive light,
  not degrading him or her for reasons that are over
  the heads of the children (such as infidelity or
  financial reverses)?

- Am I making sure that my (new) spouse has a positive
  role in our children's lives? Am I building a strong
  foundation for respect and affection, even if the
  children are not ready to love the stepparent yet?

- Do I make certain my children see their dad/mom?
  Do I manage to keep him/her involved in their lives,

even if we are no longer together? Do I treat him/
her with respect as their other parent?

- Are the children aware of each other's rights and
responsibilities? Do I make certain that normal family
bickering has an undercurrent of love and
tolerance?

- Do I encourage my children to be individuals and
to follow their own inclinations and work toward their
own goals? Or do I treat all the children the same,
involving them in the same activities for my own
convenience?

- Do I encourage my children to know their aunts,
uncles, cousins, stepfamilies? How involved are they
with relatives outside of the immediate family?

- Are grandparents left out of my child's life? Are
they too involved in it? Does my child pit the
grandparents against the parents?

- Am I getting too much conflicting information from
my in-laws? Are my children caught in a tug-of-
war between differing parenting philosophies? How
can I tell my in-laws (or my own parents) when they
are involving themselves too much (or not enough)
or treating my children in ways I don't approve
of?

- Should all my children be treated relatively the same,
or should allowances be made for differences in sex,
age, and temperament? What are those differences
and how should they be handled?

- Is there one family member who is the Final Boss?
  Does one parent have the final say in
  responsibilities and discipline? How can I decide which
  parent that should be? Should we divide up areas of
  our children's lives and split the responsibilities on
  those?

Phases and Stages: The Stress and Strains of Child Rearing Never End

Children are always going through a different developmental stage, each with its own particular stresses and parents are forced to live through those stages with their children, going through the trials and tribulations side by side with them.

The Early Years. There is a proverb that says, "Beware of what you ask for, because you might get it." Any parent who has counted off the days until her child was old enough to go to school, and then felt bereft when he finally trotted away, knows the wisdom of that proverb. When the child is old enough to leave home, everything changes. You are both more and less free than you have been for the past five years. You have more freedom because you have those extra hours every day when your child is away at school. But you may be less free because you have to accommodate your child's (or children's) schedule. You may have to arrange to drop him off or pick him up. You used to be able to put your child or children in the car and go; now you have to consider whether you will be back in time to fulfill your carpool duties.

Your spouse may see your new free time as completely free,

not understanding you still have to take care of many parts of child rearing. Even though your child isn't there, you still have to do his laundry, make his meals, clean up after him (again and again), schedule his doctor's appointments, and the like. There may be less time than you would like because now you have to help with the homework, perhaps help out at school, and schedule everything around the school day.

With the child away, you may feel at a loss for a while. You worry how your child is doing without you, whether he misses you as much as you miss him. You may become a little resentful of the fact that your child sees other people in his life as more important than you (or so it seems to you). You hear him talk about his teacher and friends, and maybe you get a little jealous. Your spouse, who didn't spend as much time with the child at home as you did, might not understand your feelings of loss and be less sympathetic than you would like.

The Middle Years. The middle years are a time of endless energy and activity. No part of life is left untouched. Children aren't driving cars yet, and their activities range from school to piano lessons to soccer practice. Children are also gaining a sense of independence and wanting to exercise their own will. In other words, children need their parents more than ever, even as they begin pushing them away emotionally while learning to rely more and more on themselves.

During a child's early years, a little boy is closer to his mother than to his father, while a little girl is definitely Daddy's Little Darling. During adolescence, affiliations change. Girls turn toward their mothers, boys toward their fathers. This can be very confusing and disheartening for parents who have worked hard to make bonds with their children only to find that they have suddenly changed allegiance. A parent who has been friend and adviser feels left out and may blame his spouse for "alienation of affection." The resulting stress is not only between the parent and child but between the parents.

The Turbulent Teens. For many of us, the turbulent teen years of our children coincide with the most difficult times of our own lives. Just when our children need us, we are in the middle of building our careers or suddenly realizing that we have to start planning for our retirement. We have our own midlife evaluations (or crises) and may not have the desire or energy to deal with our temperamental teenagers.

We want our children to grow up to be strong and independent, capable of caring for themselves, but it's not easy to let go of them. When a child gets her driver's license, for example, we are suddenly not as involved in her life. We don't have to give her rides, which sounds like a good thing, but think of all the time you spend together in the car with your daughter and her friends. By playing chauffeur and keeping your ears open, you can learn a lot about your children. When you are no longer part of the ride, you may feel left out of the life as well.

With this free time comes the "obligation" to spend more time with your spouse, to become "young lovers" again. In a healthy marriage, intimacy is renewed and revitalized. But sometimes the partners have grown in opposite directions and find they have little in common anymore. This is especially true if one spouse spent all the time taking care of the children while the other worked outside the home. The at-home spouse has free time and may feel "retired" while the other spouse still goes to work each day. The outside worker may resent the retired spouse. Or, alternately, the at-home spouse may be bored and want something to do. As one husband put it, "It's not fair. For years, my wife had no time for me, just for our son. Now that our son is working out his independence, my wife wants me to take his place and be the child she lost."

And let's not forget the inherent strains of the teenage years. At this time, when children are testing their independence, they may turn to drugs or alcohol. A previously calm child may suddenly turn into a kamikaze. A mom may find her son taking a drink and ground him, only to have the father give the car keys back to him, saying, "Hey, I did the same thing at his age. Boys will be boys." It may be that one parent is better with younger children, more able to relate to them and give them nurturing and support, while the other parent is more attuned to older children and their grown-up activities. This conflict can turn the home into a battlefield, with the children in the middle.

The Partial Departure. The empty-nest syndrome is very real. After years of having three or more chairs at the breakfast table, it can be shocking to have only two. After years of feeding a hungry teenager, shopping for two older people who don't go into a feeding frenzy every afternoon can seem downright dull. Some parents blame the other for the child's departure: "If you hadn't gotten this macho stuff into his head, he'd be willing to live here with us instead of in that rat trap apartment with those other boys." "If you hadn't insisted he go to your old college, he could have gone to the community college and lived here at home." Parents naturally miss their children and turn their frustrations and loneliness toward one another.

There's pressure on the spouses to begin new lives now as well. Society seems to decree that once the children have gone away, the parents can begin all over, getting to know each other, traveling, spending more time together. What happens if you don't want to spend more time together, if you were comfortable with the way things were? You may feel guilty that you don't seem to like your spouse as much as you used to and that you miss your children more than you think you should. If you and your spouse have each other and still feel lonely, you may begin to wonder whether something is wrong with your marriage.

Balancing Career and Children

Helping our children learn to be capable and loving people can certainly be a full-time job, but for many of us, of course, it is not. Today, there are more adults who work outside of the home, balancing career and children, than there are stay-at-home full-time parents.

"I love my job," said Debbie, beaming with pride as she talked about the satisfaction and excitement if offered her. "But I never seem to be able to pull myself out of the office before 5:30 and sometimes later. Then, I'm still on a treadmill. I frantically rush through the store grabbing things for dinner, and then dash to Johnny's day care to fetch him. I rush home to start dinner and restore the house to some semblance of order. It's never done; there's a pile of laundry just waiting, mail to open and read, phone calls from friends and family to return, the need to find a book I recommended to someone who has called three times to see if I found it for her, and let's not forget the briefcase of work to be read and dealt with by the next morning. When Johnny comes to me with a little scrape or is fussy, it's sometimes more than I can handle. I start with the intention that I'm going to be one of those parents who keeps the television off or at least keeps it to a minimum, but when I get home, setting my child in front of the television for a blessed forty-five minutes of time for myself seems really nice. I know it's not what he needs and that I'm not a good parent at these times, but I need that downtime from being pulled in so many different directions."

Debbie isn't alone; the U.S. Department of Labor reports that more than thirty-eight million American children have moms who are employed full-time outside the home. That's 62 percent of all children under the age of eighteen.

Many parents struggle with the ongoing debate of quality versus quantity in the time they spend with their children. How much time do children need, and how does the amount vary at different stages of childhood? For parents of a very young child, this issue translates into the stressor of the work/stay-at-home dilemma. Just a generation or two ago, parental roles were more defined. Fathers went to work; mothers, in most cases, remained at home to take care of the children full-time. Today, many households need incomes from both parents just to make ends meet. Nearly 61 percent of women are head of a household, supporting the family all alone. Even if the family could do well on only one income, often the woman chooses to work to enrich her own life.

Working women hire child care or send the children off to day care, then worry whether they are doing the right thing. Is the care their children are getting damaging in any way? Is it as nourishing and fulfilling as it must be? And not all working mothers can afford child care. A national survey in 1990 by the U.S. Department of Education found that 44 percent of five- to twelve-year-olds whose mothers were employed had no care arrangements at all. Estimates of latchkey children range from two million to fifteen million, possibly 45 percent of all elementary school children.

Stay-at-home mothers may fret that they are not fulfilling their own potential or are depriving their children of the extras that a second income could provide, or they may feel embarrassed about being "just a housewife."

Both groups of mothers have to deal with criticism from those in the other camp. Both wonder if they are effective parents and if they are modeling the behavior that will serve their children well—now and in their adult years.

Working parents ask themselves:

- Am I being unfair to my children? Do I spend enough quality time with them? Just what is quality time? Do dinners count? Drives to school? How do I know if my children are being slighted?

- Does my working hurt my children, either by taking too much time away from them, by making me distant and aloof because my work is on my mind, or by making me so frazzled at the end of the day that I can't devote the time and attention to my kids that I would like?

- Am I choosing the right day care for my children? Do they get good care while I am away? How can

I be sure? Would they really tell me if there were problems (and can they articulate them?), or would they be afraid to do so?

- Am I being selfish by working full time? Am I putting my own needs ahead of those of my children? Is it true that I am a better parent when I am fulfilled as a person, or is that just an attempt at self-justification?

- Is my rushing off to work in the morning making me lose some of the joys of parenthood, including the small talk at the breakfast table, the loving hug good-bye? Am I so involved in what I am going to be doing at work that day that I ignore what my children are going to be doing at their "jobs" in the classroom?

Parents who do not work outside the home ask themselves:

- Is my being a full-time parent having a negative effect on my children? Do they resent me for being old-fashioned and staying at home?

- Is our not having a second income hurting my children because they can't have as many of the things as their friends from two-career families have? If we cannot place our children in enrichment activities that my working would allow us to afford, such as piano lessons or gymnastics, will my children be as competent as their peers who have had these experiences?

- If I don't work, or if I work reduced hours, am
  I sending the wrong message to my children? Am I
  bringing them up to think working is unimportant?
  Do they think of me as lazy if I stay at home?

- Will my children respect me less because "all my
  friends' moms work; my mom just stays at home"?

The Spouse as Parent

My friend Dianne told me, "I had a child because I was madly
in love with my husband and pregnancy seemed like the ulti-
mate sign of our passion. Then this child was born . . . and I
had no time or energy for my husband and our passion. I loved
being pregnant—I can't say that I love being a parent!" What
happens when you miss the life you had B.C.—Before Children? Time—and lots of it—with a spouse is so important, yet
meeting the needs of our children eats up that time. We begin
to wonder how the marriage will stand up when it lacks time
and attention. We notice the strain of children on the relationship. Most of us love our children more than anything in the
world, but we admit that there are days when we would like to
have some time to ourselves.

Parents begin to ponder questions such as:

- Did I anticipate the changes parenthood would make
  in my relationship with my spouse? Were the changes
  better or worse than I thought they would be?

- How is my spouse doing as a parent? What does
  he or she think about my own parenting skills? What

happens if we are disappointed in each other? What do I do if my wonderful spouse is a bad parent?

• Are my spouse and I competing for the affection of our children? Is some competition healthy, or does it hurt both ourselves and our children?

• Do my spouse and I have a basic parenting philosophy that we have discussed, and tried to implement, or are we really winging it? What do we do if our philosophies are radically different? How do we decide who is right and who is wrong?

My Husband, "Dad"; My Wife, "Mom"

Parenting can change how you see yourself, your spouse, and your relationship. Instead of hearing the sultry whisper, "Lover, come here, I want you . . ." you hear glass breaking, a child's cry, and the exasperated voice of your spouse bellowing, "Mom, come here, we need you!" Somehow it lacks romance. The pet names you had for each other have been replaced with Mommy and Daddy. You may begin to worry that you are not spending enough time on the relationship.

According to Alfie Kohn in "Making the Most of Marriage," maintaining a happy marriage is particularly difficult for couples with differing views on parenting. Dorothy had what she describes as a wonderful relationship with her husband. The two of them were always doing things together or "double dating" with other couples. They had a full and enjoyable life. When their baby was born, both parents were thrilled, and they spent most of the first few months at home with their son. They enjoyed watching Lennie grow and develop. But as Dorothy continued to spend all her time with Lennie, Jay felt excluded. His wife and son seemed to be a complete unit, with no space left for him. Although he told himself his feelings were silly, Jay was lonely. A little uncomfortable about going out with the couples who were Dorothy's and his mutual friends, Jay began making new friends. Soon he was spending a lot of time with these new friends, playing handball after work, golf on the weekends, and poker every chance he got.

As Jay began spending more time away from his wife and son, it was Dorothy's turn to feel lonely. She also felt resentful. "Jay is so wrapped up in his friends. He ignores me and our son. It's not fair. Jay has almost a whole new life that I know nothing about. I haven't even met some of his friends. And he has a new support system that I don't have. He can talk about adult things with them, real frustrations and problems. Lennie's gurgling, no matter how adorable, isn't *all* that I need. I want to talk to an *adult!*"

Dorothy and Jay were going through a normal stage in marriage, the stressful time of adjusting to a new baby. In his book *Creative Marriage*, Mel Krantzler identifies and examines six natural passages of "marriages within a marriage" and discusses the many special demands made by children through each stage of growth and development. Understanding and managing those passages, fortified by the mutual love felt for the child, can make a couple's relationship even stronger. But spouses need to make sure that they still are a couple. Couples will ask themselves:

- Has my romance taken a back seat to parenting?
- Have I given up on my appearance? Do I even resemble

that person my spouse used to describe as sexy?
Do I smell more like Baby No. 2 than Chanel
No. 5?

• Do I buy things for the kids with the money I used
to spend on my spouse? Do I still buy Dad those
playfully wild boxer shorts? Do I still remember
to buy Mom flowers for no reason at all?

• Do I spend on my children the money I used to spend
on myself? Have I given up going to the beauty
salon or the manicurist, feeling that doing so is
frivolous and not quite right for a parent?

• Are my spouse and I spending enough time together,
or has our personal time been completely taken
over by the children? Do we have any privacy, or
do the children invade even our bedroom and our
bubble baths?

• When we are together, do my spouse and I talk only
about the kids and not about ourselves and our
relationship? Do we see each other as parents first
and as lovers second?

The Challenge of Balancing Parenting and Self-Fulfillment
What happens when you begin to resent your children—not as
individuals (you admit that they are great kids), but just because
they consume or utterly change your life? Maybe you fret that
you are "nothing more than Brian's mom." Jody, a teacher for
nearly a decade, was proud of her excellent professional reputation and felt her future was secure. Then her baby was born pre-

mature and with a congenital heart defect. Because the baby needed extra care, she stayed home full-time. The love of her baby couldn't stop her from wondering whether her teaching skills would be obsolete by the time she returned to the classroom. She began to feel she was "just a housewife" and couldn't call herself anything else. She worried that she was becoming like the characters in the Bruce Springsteen song "Glory Days," who only wanted to talk about the good old days. Fretted Jody, "It's not whether or not you love your children; it's all a matter of feeling personally unfulfilled."

Parents like Jody may ask themselves:

- Are my own goals and dreams unfulfilled? Am I ignoring the plans I made for myself, postponing everything "until Whitney is grown" and then resenting the child for that? Do I feel the years slipping away from me with nothing productive done? Are my friends passing me by in their careers?

- Do I resent having to place the needs of my children before my own? Have I grown irritated at having to buy new clothes for rapidly growing children instead of something for myself?

- Does it seem as if there is no end to parenting? That there's no one time when I can sit back and say, "That's it, I've done a good job, I'm through now"? How do I know when I'm "through parenting"? Do I still owe my twenty-year-old child financial support if it's needed? Are parents expected always to put their child's needs before their own?

• Have I lost my self-esteem and given up on myself because I feel I will be hurting my children if I take time to build onto my own life?

• How do I deal with the lack of privacy that comes with being responsible for others on a full-time basis? How much time can I take for myself and my concerns without feeling I am slighting my children?

• How have I changed? Am I enjoying how I have changed because of my parenting role?

Taking time for oneself is necessary. It's also often difficult to do. When my daughter Jennifer was young, I was feeling a bit cooped up one day. I wanted to go out, but I had to be home with my daughter. The doorbell rang. A friend of my daughter's stood there and said, as she had said a hundred times before, "Can Jennifer come out to play?" I shook my head and said, "No, honey, Jennifer is doing her homework. But my work is all done and I'd love to come and play with you." Anita looked at me as if I were crazy and stammered, "You can't come out to play; you're the mother!" She giggled and ran away. Yet sometimes parents want to go and play, too. Sometimes we momentarily pine for the lives we had when we had only ourselves and our spouses to think of, when our own needs came first.

How Well Do You Handle Stress? Three Quizzes

Not all of the stress adults experience is a result of dealing with the needs and concerns of children. We have our own needs, concerns, and fears that contribute to our own stress levels.

Children learn from what they see; parents teach through their actions. Though we may say, "Do as I say," children often do what we *do*. That's all the more reason to be working toward managing your own response to stress.

How do you respond to stress? Do you make stress an ally, drawing vitality from it? How to you manage when the stresses and strains of life loom large? What strategies do you employ for coping with stress? For example, do you use exercise as a way to alleviate stress, or do you avoid exercise, especially when you're tense? Do you let interruptions and the needs of others dominate your needs, or are you assertive about what you need?

Begin by taking stock. As you accumulate insights into your behavior and your response to stress, you begin to build a reservoir of wisdom, successful strategies to use when adjusting to stress-producing people and stress-producing situations. You begin to see more clearly your own contribution to stress. This stress may be negative, working against you, or positive, working for you.

One of the central concepts in coping with stress is to recognize the role expectations play in giving us a feeling of either gratification or frustration. Whether we call our activities exhausting work or relaxing play depends largely upon our own attitude toward what we do. We need to be on friendly terms with our lives. You will fare best if you make a point of being flexible, lead a healthy and balanced life, do not take yourself too seriously, are not afraid to learn new skills in dealing with stress, approach change with zest and zeal, and are not intimidated in seeking professional counseling or other outside help when you recognize a need for support in coping with the difficult moments in life.

Just as an educator under stress passes anxiety along to his or her students, stressed-out parents put some of their anxiety on their children. With their heightened sensitivity, children are especially vulnerable to the feelings of their parents. If you show them that you accept stress as a part of life, can recognize when you have exceeded your stress threshold, and have developed coping strategies and behaviors to deal with it, you send the message to your children that stress can be dealt with effectively.

Not everyone goes out of his way to avoid stress. In fact, there are those who actually look for stress, who thrive under pressure! Maybe you wait until the last minute before you begin a task, thereby creating pressure for yourself to complete it on time. If that's your style, it could be that you're a stress seeker. To find out, take the following quiz.

Are You a Stress Seeker?

Using a rating of 4 to mean "Always," 3 to mean "Frequently," 2 to mean "Sometimes," and 1 to mean "Never," rate yourself as to how you typically react in each of the situations listed.

_____ 1. Do you have a tendency to put things off until the last minute and then frantically rush to get them done?

_____ 2. Do you thrive on situations in which there is pressure, competition, tension, or risk?

_____ 3. Do you find stress or tension to be a driving force behind your major accomplishments?

_____ **4.** Do you feel exhilarated or energized after accomplishing a difficult task or closing an important business deal?

_____ **5.** Do you enjoy novelty and challenge in your work?

_____ **6.** Do you have a tendency to see obstacles as challenges rather than headaches?

_____ **7.** Do you seek ways to improve yourself or your performance in your field?

_____ **8.** In general, would you classify yourself as a risk taker rather than a risk avoider?

_____ **9.** Are you willing to give up job security for job challenge?

_____ **10.** Are you able to quickly "come down," physically and emotionally, after a tension-producing event?

_____ **11.** Do you seek action-oriented vacations?

_____ **12.** In your leisure time do you pursue activities in which there is a certain amount of danger or risk, such as skydiving or rock climbing?

Scoring. Add up your total score. If is between 36 and 48, you are a stress seeker who enjoys excitement and exhilaration. You actually look around for and create a high stress level to propel you to action. You like stress. You *thrive* on it! If your score is between 24 and 35, you probably like things to go smoothly; you like harmony and strive to keep things in perspective, to balance your life in order to stay on an even keel. A score between 12 and 23 indicates that you are likely to avoid stress and seek security instead. You don't like to be charged with emotion and find that such conditions sap your energy.

Regardless of whether we rush to meet stress head-on or cower in a corner hoping to lead as placid a life as possible, some stress will find us. If we hope to grow as individuals, we have to put ourselves on the edge at one time or another. This could mean taking chances in our careers, marriages, or activities. We don't grow until we live on the edge of our experience ... and being perched on that edge can be very stressful at times.

Each of us has developed measures and patterns for taking care of ourselves. The following assessment is a tool to help you recognize your stress resilience. It can help you determine how vulnerable you are to stress and point to areas where you may need to learn skills to encounter the effects of stress. Answer each question from 1 to 5, with 1 being "Very Often" and 5 being "Very Rarely." Don't give the "correct" answer; give the answer that reflects your current situation.

How Do You Cope with Stress?

_____ 1. I'm less than ten pounds overweight or underweight.

_____ 2. I have at least one sit-down, relaxed meal a day and my diet is well balanced.

_____ 3. I do aerobic exercise at least twenty minutes each day for three days a week.

_____ 4. I get about eight hours of sleep at night.

_____ 5. I have fewer than three cups of caffeinated drinks (coffee, tea, soft drinks) a day.

_____ 6. I have no more than two or three alcoholic drinks a week.

_____ 7. I smoke fewer than five cigarettes a day.

_____ 8. I consider myself in general good health and have no specific health worries.

_____ 9. I make a point of taking a few minutes a day for downtime, time to relax and unwind.

_____ 10. I make a point of doing at least one activity a day just for me, something I enjoy.

_____ 11. I make enough money to cover my living expenses and have no serious financial worries.

_____ 12. I have a close or best friend with whom I can discuss my day on a regular basis.

_____ 13. I have a wide variety of interesting friends and acquaintances with whom I share enjoyable activities.

_____ 14. I belong to a club or social organization that makes me feel accepted and wanted.

_____ 15. I have good communication with my family or with the people in my household; we can talk out little annoyances before they become serious problems.

_____ 16. I have a supportive family and know I can count on my relatives to help if I am ever in serious trouble.

_____ 17. I "blow up" and get matters off my chest, then forget the matter and go on relatively easily.

_____ 18. I am able to give and take love and affection.

_____ 19. I have at least one person in my life who tells me regularly that he or she loves me.

_____ 20. I am comforted by my spiritual beliefs.

Scoring. Add up the numbers you assigned to each statement. If your total is under 50, congratulations! You have a strong resistance to stress and are probably handling the events in your life well. If your total is between 51 and 70, you are vulnerable to stress and should be more aware of what stressors are in your life and how well or poorly you handle them. If your score is over 70, you are extremely vulnerable to stress and need to reevaluate your life-style or possibly talk with someone, such as a counselor, to help you get a better balance in your life.

Are You a Candidate for Burnout?

Now that you have identified how well or poorly you take care of yourself, it's time to go one step further and examine your potential for burnout. Read the following statements and answer either "not at all," "rarely," "occasionally," "usually," or "very often."

Physical
1. I have headaches, colds, flu. _____
2. I suffer from backaches. _____
3. I am in a hurry, rushing. _____
4. I have digestive problems
(upset stomach, diarrhea). _____
5. My blood pressure is high. _____
6. I feel tired. _____

Behavioral

7. I am impatient with others. _____

8. I am irritable in a wide
variety of settings. _____

9. I am critical of others. _____

10. I have trouble accepting
criticism. _____

11. I complain to others but
do not take action to
improve a situation. _____

12. I am demanding of myself
and of others. _____

Emotional

13. I have to push myself to
keep going on a project. _____

14. I use anger or sarcasm when
making a point. _____

15. I tell myself, "I am really
not doing as well as I could." _____

16. I doubt that I can get the
job done. _____

17. I do not believe that
others really like me. _____

18. I fly off the handle. _____

Intellectual

19. I have been forgetting important dates/ assignments. _____

20. I find it hard to concentrate. _____

21. I find myself daydreaming. _____

22. I find it difficult to make decisions. _____

23. I put off important tasks. _____

24. I have too many things on my mind at once. _____

Organizational

25. My relationships at work are not satisfying. _____

26. I do not get support for my decisions. _____

27. I do not believe others can do the job as well as I can. _____

28. I feel tense at work. _____

29. I feel confused about what I am really supposed to be doing on the job. _____

30. The time pressures at work do not allow me to complete tasks properly. _____

Scoring. Go back and count up your points. Assign yourself 0 points for each "Not at all," 1 point for each "Rarely," 2 points for each "Occasionally," 3 points for each "Usually," and 4 points for each "Very often."

Your Burnout Range

0–29 = Safe. You seem to be reacting to life events in a way that does not deplete your resources or your ability to take care of yourself.

30–59 = Average. You could be taking better care of yourself. Your standards for yourself and others are usually high, and this causes you to have frequent run-ins with yourself.

60–89 = Warning. You are very close to burning out. You are probably encountering many difficulties and disappointments and having a hard time adjusting to events. Your resources are being depleted faster than you can replace them.

90–120 Overload! Overload! If your score is in this range, you are already burned out and need to stop and reassess your life. You may want to get some outside, professional help because your life has become more than you can handle. Take steps now, before your body and mind find the stress levels intolerable.

How to Relieve the Stress of Parenting

There are no simple steps to make things easier in our struggle to juggle and balance our lives. But parents can do some things that will likely relieve the stress of caretaking and the strain of coping with the demands of raising children.

1. Take care of yourself. All too often it is the personal care and fitness of the parent that becomes expendable. As a young working parent striving to handle a demanding career while remaining responsive to my daughter and to my husband, both of whom I considered my first priority, I found myself constantly erasing and rescheduling the time I had allotted for my aerobic workouts. Time at the gym seemed like the most expendable activity on my calendar. Then one day I landed in the hospital with an ulcer in the making, and I learned the hard way that if I didn't take care of myself, I wouldn't be able to take care of those I loved and those to whom I was responsible. Parents need to schedule time for activities that allow for physical and emotional release, and to guard that time as necessary to both themselves and others. Because we respect and value ourselves, we must take care of ourselves. Doing so is a sign of commitment to our parenting effectiveness.

2. Keep reading and learning. Parents need to keep learning about what's ahead in the next age and stage of their child's development. The field of psychology as it relates to children and family health has grown in scope and depth over the past few years. Keep reading and learning and working toward building healthy relationships with your children. Doing so can help both you and your child know what to expect at each age. And it can help you determine what to do and where to turn should you need assistance and support.

3. Develop or join a parenting support group. Talking with other parents and finding out how they are coping with the challenges of raising children can be a good support system. A word of caution: Choose to be with parents who are positive and enjoy their children. The goal is to enrich your own parenting experiences, to enhance your joy in parenting your children.

4. Value the relationship with your children's other parent. One of the most important factors contributing to raising happy and emotionally healthy children is the modeling of these elements in their parents. The quality of attention you give your children is important; it's necessary for the vibrancy of your coparenting relationship as well. Treat your children's other parent with courtesy, respect, and affection. These are necessary ingredients in keeping the relationship a loving one, and you can be sure your children are watching and learning.

5. Seek assistance when necessary. A professional who is skilled and objective can help you examine your concerns about parenting and can be of immense help at a time of crisis, whether between you and your child or you and your parenting partner. A professional can also help your child work through a crisis that is beyond your own ability to help.

6. Lighten up and have fun. All too often parents focus on the work and obligations of parenting and forget that parenting can be one of the most delightful experiences in life. Decide to enjoy it. How much you enjoy it is first about increasing the value of parenting in your own mind. My friend who decided that his children were not a liability and in fact were his "portfolio" made an important discovery. It began by his awareness of the importance of his children. Once he realized that, it was easy to develop skills in being a good parent and to do those things that helped his children become loving and competent people.

7. Learn to manage your response to stress. If you feel you need to learn better ways to manage your response to the stress, strains, and pressures of parenting, consider learning more about stress reduction either by reading about or by taking a course in stress management. Generally you can find stress management courses offered at local junior colleges or at adult education centers. The reference section at the back of this book lists a number of excellent reading resources for parents.

Self-Awareness Is Job One
Parents are the most important role models children have. When we take the time to evaluate our own stress levels, we send our children a message that we recognize stress and its importance in our lives. By understanding the different types of stresses that are common to adults, we know what to expect and don't fret that we are somehow abnormal or haven't quite mastered this business of being a grown-up. We know that there are certain stresses, both positive and negative, that most adults are subject to. Because different people react to stress in different ways, it's good to know which type of stress-seeker you are, in order to develop a plan for coping. In short, to learn how to help your children manage their stress constructively, acceptably,

and positively, you must first know your own stresses and your reactions to them.

Communication between parents and children—talking openly about how we are feeling about the stress and strains of managing the many hats we are wearing—is a first step in getting the support and assistance we need to minimize the toll of stress.

Stress Prevention and Intervention Techniques

Chapter 9

TALKING WITH YOUR
CHILDREN ABOUT STRESS

Even though you strive to give your children the benefit of all your knowledge and experience, there comes a time when they must begin to maneuver through the maze of life and learn to cope successfully on their own. If they are to maintain a high level of emotional and physical well-being, they too must learn to manage the stress and strains they are likely to experience. By helping your children develop skills and strategies for managing stress, you can decrease the toll stress takes on them and increase their psychological hardiness and resilience.

This chapter and the next one include sample scenarios that illustrate stressful experiences and stress-reducing skills that are useful in helping young people manage their response to stress. Depending on your child's age, you may have to simplify or add more sophistication to a given scenario to fit your child's ability level. If you can draw from something going on in your child's life right now, so much the better. The more true-to-life the story is, the more your child will identify with it and be open to your suggestions and the skills you are teaching.

Should you wish to expand upon these or related stress management skills, you may want to examine my previous books *Problem Solving Skills for Children* (for ages 3–10), *A Stress Management Guide for Young People* (for ages 10–20), or *You and Self-Esteem: A Book for Young People* (ages 10–20). These books are designed for young people themselves and have proved to be effective. These and a number of other excellent sources are listed in the resource section of this book.

Discussing Stress and Stress Management with Your Child

Your first task is to make sure your children understand what stress is and how a stressor affects them. For most children, definitions work best when put in the context of their everyday activities. In defining stress, begin by reading the examples of Lila and Tawny found on page 83. Ask your children which girl did the best job of handling the situation, and why. They should find it pretty easy to see that Tawny resolved her dilemma a bit better than Lila. Let your children freely talk about why they feel as they do, and don't be too judgmental as they do so. The goal is to get your children talking about some of the pressures they are feeling.

Children also need to know that we *all* feel stress at times. At times we simply have too many things to do but must still get them done. We may feel overwhelmed, but we cannot let such feelings debilitate us. Sometimes we may be fearful that we won't know the best way to do something, that we won't make the very best choice, or that we won't have the courage to carry out the decision we know is best. Feeling stressed is only natural. Children need to know that stress is a cue to cope; when we feel stress, it means something isn't right and we must take *positive action* to alleviate it.

Your second task, then, is to reassure your children that managing stress involves skills that can be learned. Children of all ages need to know that they can learn ways to reduce the fears they are feeling and that they can manage the stresses and strains that sometimes seem overwhelming. Teach your children how to do this in ways that are positive and that affirm respect and care for their bodies. For example, if my daughter had a tension-related headache, I would suggest that she get on her bicycle and go for a ride in order to alleviate the stress, rather than take a Tylenol to dull the pain. Again, modeling is important. Your children are likely to pick up your habits and do as you *do*, not necessarily as you say.

Is Your Child Experiencing Stress?

To begin to understand your child's stress, get an idea of how stressful he considers his life to be. This may differ from your own impression. For example, you may believe that your child has good socialization skills and makes friends easily, but your child may feel that other children dislike him. If your child feels that way, it can be a source of stress, regardless of your sense that he has good socialization skills.

Not all stress is transitory. Some things cannot be changed or altered; for example, your child's school life will not get less stressful. In fact, each year there will be additional demands on your child's ability to manage the school' agenda. For some stresses, your child must learn ways to manage his or her stress responses. It's helpful, then, to know exactly what is the cause or origin of a stress.

The *Stress Test for Young People*, which follows, can assist you in determining how much stress your child feels, and in what areas. This information can then help you find and apply appropriate techniques to aid your child in stress management. For example, you may think that your child is stressed out about his schoolwork, when the real culprit is not the school agenda or the amount of homework assigned but your child's having to confront a bully in one or more of his classes. Thus, the task becomes to help your child find ways to alleviate the stress of a personality clash, rather than helping him better manage the job of being a student.

Have your child do the assessment alone if he or she is able to do so. If not, read each item to your child and mark the response that represents your child's feelings.

A Stress Test for Young People

Read the following statements and answer either "often," "sometimes," or "never."

1. In the last month have you felt any of the following symptoms: dizziness, painfully cold hands or feet, headaches, sore muscles, stomach aches? _____

2. In the last month have you had crying spells, feelings of being angry, or moodiness? _____

3. Do you have recurring nightmares? _____

4. Do you experience pain in your neck, back, arms? _____

5. Do you feel depressed or unhappy? _____

6. Do you worry? _____

7. Do you feel anxious even though you don't know why? _____

8. Are you impatient with your friends or family members? _____

9. Do you dwell on things you did but shouldn't have done? _____

10. Do you have difficulty
focusing on your schoolwork?   _____
11. Do you worry about what
others think of you?   _____
12. Are you bored?   _____
13. Do you have serious
conflicts with others?   _____
14. Do you find yourself
irritable and argumentative?   _____
15. Are you as popular with
your friends as you would
like?   _____
16. Are you doing as well in
school as you would like?   _____
17. Do you feel you can live up
to the expectations of your
parents, teachers, and activity
leaders?   _____
18. Do you feel your parents
understand your problems and
are supportive?   _____
19. Are you satisfied with the
way you look?   _____
20. Do you have trouble with
any of your teachers, coaches, or
activity leaders?   _____
21. Do you worry that your
friends might be against you?   _____

22. Do you think you eat more
(or less) than you should? _____

23. Do you make strong
demands on yourself? _____

24. Do you feel that the limits
imposed on you by your
parents, teachers, or coaches are
justified? _____

25. Do your parents, teachers,
or coaches criticize you? _____

26. Is there anyone who is
overly competitive with you? _____

27. Have you suffered a severe
illness or injury in the last
year? _____

28. Do you experience conflict
or peer pressure to engage in
certain activities? _____

29. Have you recently moved to
a new home, neighborhood, or
school? _____

30. Is it difficult for you to say
no to a request? _____

31. Do you feel ill after an
emotional upset? _____

The questions on this informal assessment are relatively straightforward. They are not intended as a diagnosis but rather as a tool to help you determine if your child has a relatively low, moderate, or high level of stress. If your child responds with a "sometimes" or "never" to many of these questions, it doesn't mean that his or her life is devoid of stress but rather that your child, in spite of minor worries and concerns, has found ways to deal successfully with the stress, strains, and pressures in his or her life.

If the level of stress reported by this test seems moderate or high, you'll want to help your child learn new methods to better deal with his or her stress. Talking with your child's educators, school nurse, or counselor can also add to the picture of how stressed your child feels, and what may be of benefit in helping your child acquire management skills.

Explaining Stress to Your Child

Begin by explaining to your children that the things that cause stress are called *stressors*. Give examples of stressors, such as:

- having a disagreement with your parents
- being ignored by the cool kids at school or having someone at school make fun of you
- feeling skinny, fat, ugly, or dumb
- not having enough money to buy what you want
- not having permission from your parents to go somewhere you want to go
- being unable to do something you really want to do

- being angry at your friends or siblings, or having them angry at you
- not getting a good grade on a paper, especially when you thought you would

Explain that not everyone has the same stressors. You might say: "Maybe your friend gets stressed out about something but you don't. What you think is stressful may not bother your friend. For example, maybe you get very stressed when you have to stand in front of the class and give a report, whereas that doesn't bother your friend at all. Maybe you think it's fun to jump off the high diving board at the pool, but your best buddy starts shaking just thinking about doing so. Everyone is different."

Here is a three-part exercise that will help your children put stressors in perspective. First, have your children generate a list of things that have stressed them recently. To be sure that the lists have variety, ask them to list some things that are physical (climbing up the rope in gym class), some that are related to the family (having to share a room with a sibling), and some that are related to friends (having a new kid come into class and "take away" friends). Have your children identify three or four things in each category.

Second, help your kids list three or four situations that caused them stress a few months ago (if they are young) or in the past two years (if they are older). For example, a child might have been very nervous about crossing the street by himself but now does so with confidence. An older child might laugh when he looks back and sees how nervous he was at his first "boy-girl" party.

Finally, have your children make a list of things that cause others stress but don't cause them stress. You might tell them a story such as the following one. In it, even very young children can see two very different responses to the same situation.

Stephen and Rick
Stephen gets to his locker before he notices that his keys are missing. He retraces his steps from the time he entered the school building but doesn't find the keys anywhere. He returns to his locked car and notices the keys in the ignition. Now that he knows where the keys are, he begins to generate alternatives—thinking of all the ways he can solve the problem. He decides to call his mom at work to ask her to bring him an extra set of car keys. Though he is annoyed that he will have to change his lunch-hour plans and worries about the inconvenience that he might cause his mother, he returns to the school building to call her before hurrying off to class.

Like Stephen, Rick gets to his locker before he notices that his keys are missing. But unlike Stephen's calm, Rick has a totally different reaction. He frantically asks his friends if they have seen his keys and gets irritated when they don't become involved in helping him locate them. He gets angry at his best friend, Norman, because his friend doesn't seem as concerned as Rick would like him to be. Panicking and upset, he is unable to think clearly enough to trace his steps back to the car. Unable to think of anything but locating the keys, he forgets to get the necessary books and materials from his locker before his next class. For the next three hours he cannot concentrate on his school activities. He is demanding and impatient with his friends, short and unfriendly toward his teachers, and unable to be productive in his classes. It's not long before he gets a headache and feels nauseated. He is frustrated and anxious.

The goal is to show your children that while each young man was in the same stressful predicament, each responded differently. Rick's *reaction* to the stressful event produced a debilitating result and a negative outcome. Stephen's *reaction* to the stressful event showed good problem-solving skills and had a positive outcome. Ask your child how he or she would have reacted in the situation above.

What Are the Effects of Stress?

Now you have helped your children identify what stress is, and what situations stress them personally. The next step in working with your children is to make them aware of how stress affects them. Go through the following lists with your children. Discuss each effect of stress in terms they relate to personally. For example, if the effect is "I feel my stomach churning," talk about the time that your child had to take a big spelling test and couldn't eat breakfast that morning because his stomach was so upset. This exercise can also help *you* become more aware of the effects that stress has been having on your children and more alert to future signs of stress. By discussing stress effects with your kids, you will know which ones they consider very important.

THE PHYSICAL EFFECTS
When I am stressed, my body reacts. Do I:

- feel my muscles getting tense?
- have cold or sweaty hands?
- feel my stomach churning, as if I have to throw up?
- go the bathroom a lot more frequently?
- feel my heart beating really hard?
- get very tired?
- get so wound up I can't sleep?
- lose my appetite?
- eat way too much, especially junk food?

What other physical effects can you and your children think of?

THE EMOTIONAL EFFECTS
When I am stressed, my emotions change. Do I:

- cry easily?
- feel I want to hit something or someone?
- giggle a lot, and at the wrong times?
- worry all the time?
- lose confidence in myself?
- get angry at little things?

- not care about anything, even what I look like?
- get quiet, refuse to talk to anyone, sulk?

What other emotional effects can you and your children think of?

THE BEHAVIORAL EFFECTS
When I am stressed, my behavior changes. Do I:

- have trouble concentrating?
- fib and lie a lot?
- get into fights?
- avoid doing chores or homework, or do them badly?
- ignore my friends?
- blame others for all my problems?

What other behavioral effects can you and your children think of?

Identifying How Your Children Currently Cope with Stress

So far, you have helped your children to define stress and have identified stressors unique to them. Recall with them the effects, physical, emotional, and behavioral, that stress can have on them. The next thing to do is to help your children recognize what skills they already have in place, what they currently do to cope with stress. Once they—and you—know where they are beginning, you'll be able to develop a plan to help them cope more efficiently. It's important for you to keep in mind that your child may have a personality very different from yours, may have a response to stress very different from yours, and may need a different approach to alleviate it. Again, the overall goal is to teach your child healthy ways to respond to the stress, strains, and pressure he or she is feeling. Be patient as you assess your child's current ability to manage stress and as you explore the ways to best help your child.

One way to recognize how your children cope with stress is to take them through an example of a highly stressful day. As you read aloud the following story of Rob, ask your children to be thinking of what they would do if those things happened to them. You could bring in personal examples of when that very thing, or something much like it, happened to your own children. For example, when the scenario mentions a book missing from a locker, remind your children of when they took the wrong books back to school after the weekend and had to go through the whole day without the ones they needed. What did they do then?

Rob's Day
It's Wednesday. Rob sets his alarm for 7:00 A.M. but it fails to go off. He awakens at 7:35. Because Rob is running late he skips breakfast, forgets to feed the dog, and doesn't straighten up his room.

Rob dashes for the bus but misses it. Luckily for Rob, his father has not yet left for work. Rob asks for a ride to school, and reluctantly his father agrees to take him. Since this will take his father out of his way, he too will be late for an appointment; he's annoyed at Rob because this is the second time this week that Rob has missed the bus. They ride to school in silence. This makes Rob painfully aware of how unhappy his father is with him.

Because Rob arrives late to school he must go to the office to get a late pass before he can be admitted to class. Suddenly, Rob remembers that because his father was in a bad mood Rob didn't ask him to write out an explanation for his tardiness. Afraid to call his father, and thus unable to get a pass, Rob must now sit out first period in the office.

Since he was without a pass and absent from his first class, Rob misses the science test. His teacher says he will not allow Rob to make up the test since he had an unexcused absence. This makes Rob really upset—he needed that test to improve his grade-point average in order to maintain his eligibility for the tennis team. As captain of the team, being removed because of low grades will be an embarrassment. Besides, his dad has promised to help pay for a car for Rob if his grades improve by the end of the semester. Angered about losing his chance for a car, Rob goes to his locker to get his books for second-period class. Searching for his math book, he discovers that it is missing. His locker mate has inadvertently picked up Rob's book instead of his own. Rob is frantic. When Rob failed to turn in his math assignment yesterday, his teacher warned him to bring it in the next day. Now this overdue math assignment is in the book his locker mate has, and Rob has no idea where he could be. Rather than face the teacher, Rob decides to skip math class today.

Rob's math teacher takes attendance. Because Rob is not re-

244 / Stress and Your Child

ported on the absence lists, the vice-principal calls his mother at work to inform her that her son is not in school.

The bell rings, and Rob heads off to third period. When friends tease him about his whereabouts during second period, he is rude to them. Being upset with his friends makes him feel uneasy.

Rob is standing in the lunch line when he notices his locker mate. "Hey Johnson! You took my math book, you idiot!" Rob calls out. Barney Johnson, who isn't having such a hot day either, calls Rob a bad name. Already at the end of his rope, Rob shoves his locker mate against the wall and is ready to hit him when the vice-principal stops him. Surprised to see Rob, the principal tells Rob about the call he made earlier to his mother.

Feeling really frustrated, Rob shouts at the vice-principal, demanding that he be allowed to stay in line and have lunch.

As he is led to the office, Rob thinks about what the vice-principal has in mind for him. Knowing his mother has been informed that he's not in school makes him feel even more anxious. He knows she will call his father to tell him.

Finally, at 3:15 the school day is over.

The Cycle of Stress

Rob certainly had a stressful day! One stressful event often leads to another and another, creating a *cycle of stress*, as Rob found. Use the following questions as guidelines for stimulating a discussion with your children:

- What went wrong in Rob's day?

- How did one unfortunate event led to another?

- Could Rob have stopped some of the problems from occurring? How?
- At what point should Rob have *evaluated* what was going on?
- Where should he have applied skills to stop the cycle of stress?
- What could Rob have done to better manage his day?
- Has something like this ever happened to you? How did you handle it?

Helping Your Child Learn to Assign Less Power to Stress

To help your child put stress in perspective, discuss a variety of stressful situations and their outcomes. You might say, "Do you make mountains out of molehills? Have you ever been fearful that something would happen and then it didn't? Try not to make a big deal out of small things. Think about some of the biggest fears you had last year. How many of your fears actually came true? Maybe you were afraid of being rejected by a friend when you asked him to go to a special event with you; did it actually happen, or not? If you did get turned down, was the boy nice about it? If the boy wasn't nice about it, did you handle it in a positive way? Remember the time you were afraid to return the library book because it was overdue? Did you *really* get into all that much trouble when you finally returned it, or did you find that it was manageable—that you got through it?"

As you talk with your child about his or her concerns, pick

examples from past experiences and discuss what happened, using this format:

Fear: _____

What really happened? _____

Fear: _____

What really happened? _____

Ask your child to describe a time when he saw someone who obviously was petrified and forcing herself to complete a task (for example, a singer whose voice was shaky and whose hands were white-knuckled from being clenched so tightly together). Now ask your child how he felt when the singer was done with the performance. Maybe your child pitied her while she was singing, but didn't he admire her when she was done?

Have your child describe a time when fear kept her from doing something she really wanted to do. Perhaps she wanted to try out for cheerleading squad but thought she was too clumsy or not popular enough. How did she feel about herself when she didn't even make the effort? Now have her imagine that she did go through with it.

Ask your child to describe two different scenarios, one in which your child succeeded and one in which he or she failed. Again, the goal is to help your child see that he could recover from a setback and that eventually, what he might have thought was so stressful and end-of-the-world wasn't so bad after all. *By helping your child look at stress in retrospect, you help your child to assign less power to the event.* The following questions can be used to stimulate additional discussion.

- Whom can you go to when you need help?
- Is it better to tough it out on your own and not admit your fear, or to get help?
- Do you feel others think less of you if you admit you are frightened?
- How can you stop a fear before it grows and overwhelms you?
- Do you find yourself carrying a fear from one day to the next, allowing it to grow bigger and bigger?
- How can you tell when you are making a mountain out of molehill?

Help your children feel comfortable talking about stress and the ways they experience it, and be sure to discuss how stress affects them physically, emotionally, and behaviorally. This can be enormously empowering. By removing the negative feelings of helplessness and self-criticism, children are more likely to be encouraged to learn effective ways to manage the strains they feel and to ward off impending stress efficiently. The next chapter provides a number of skills that you can use in teaching your children how to manage their response to stress.

Chapter 10

STRESS MANAGEMENT SKILLS FOR CHILDREN

Your children need to cope with their stresses. They have learned to recognize what stress is, what particular things cause them stress, what effects stress has on them, and how they usually react to stress. Now the goal is to help them develop the skills that can help minimize the negative effects of their stress.

Thinking Out Loud

One excellent way to deal with a stressful event, especially one that is anticipated and cannot be avoided (such as starting the first day of school, going to the lunchroom and hoping a classmate will sit with you, giving a speech in front of the class, taking a test, or asking someone out on a date), is to talk it

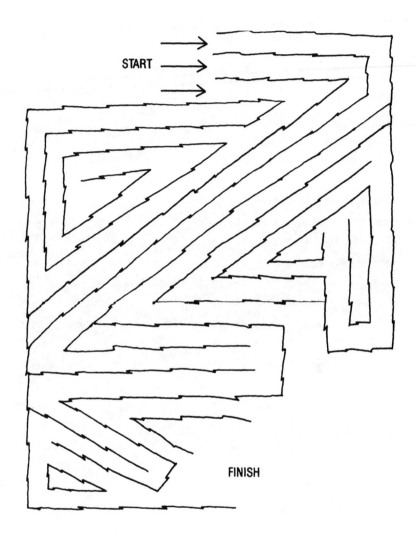

through. Thinking out loud is really a form of advance planning, a way to acquire focus and direction while maneuvering through a stressful situation.

If your child is younger than ten years old, you might use an example of getting through a maze, always a fun activity for children. Show your child how she makes each decision as she talks herself through it. Using the maze on page 249 (or any other maze), ask your child to note how she talks to herself as a way of guiding herself to the end.

Maybe your child's thinking went something like this:

"Let's see now, I need to take my pencil and find my way from the start to the finish without crossing any lines. Okay, now where should I go? What's my plan? I can go this way slowly and look ahead. Whoops, if I go down this alley it will be a wrong turn, so I should turn around and go back. No, I can't go that way, it's a dead end. Okay, this looks good. I'm making progress now. If I look ahead, I'm less likely to make a wrong turn. Oops, that lane isn't going to work either. I'll just go back to this lane and try this again. How am I doing? Okay. I'm going slowly and I'm not frustrated. I'm just about there. Aha, I did it! I did great! I made a few mistakes, but I found my way out!"

If your child is older than ten, use the following exercise. Read the short scenario together.

It's Tuesday morning. You get to school ten minutes later than usual and hear the five-minute bell ring as you run in the door. You still have to go to your locker to get your books before the first class. Sometime today you also have to set up an appointment with your counselor, stop by the library to return a book that is due this morning (and you don't want to get the same lecture that you got the last time you turned in an overdue book, so you really have to make sure you get it back *today*), go to the office to turn in a permission slip in order to be excused on Friday for a dental appointment, and buy a lunch ticket.

Having so much to do can seem overwhelming. Some kids would be tempted just to go to class and forget everything else. It's easier to do nothing, it seems, than to go through all that. But if you talk yourself through your tasks, one at a time, they don't seem so stressful. Try talking through them now.

Perhaps the thinking-out-loud went something like this:

"Let's see now, I have only five minutes until class. That means I'm going to have to concentrate on what I must get done before class. Let's see, since I'm right here, why don't I go to the office first. Where's the permission slip my mom wrote this morning? Here it is. Good, that's done. Okay, I was going to talk to my counselor, but I'd better do that during lunchtime. I'm afraid that I'll be late if I do it now. I'd better get the lunch ticket then, too. Okay, the office visit is completed so I'll swing by the library next. There's Johnny Watson. Gosh, I'd love to talk to him about last night's soccer practice. I'd better not; I just don't have the time. How am I doing? Hmmm, three minutes to go. Good, the library book is returned, now off to my locker. Let's see, 35 right, 15 left, turn it all the way around, and 25 right. Darn, I'm going too fast. I went right by 25. Okay, slow down, let's try this again—35 right, 15 left, turn it all the way around, now slowly to 25 right. Great. Okay, there's the book I need. Let me think, do I need anything else? Oh yes, I was going to have Mr. Winfield look over my science fair project before I get it typed up. I'll take that with me now. It will save me a trip later in the day. How's my time? Great, still one minute until class. I'm not going to be late. Nice going!"

Think of a day your children had recently that was crammed to overflowing with responsibilities, maybe some of which were not fulfilled. Make a list of everything that had to be done that day, then have the children talk themselves through a plan.

You Can't Always Protect Children from Stress

You can't always protect your child completely from stress, nor should you. I like the idea of what I call "psychological immunization," meaning that children become psychologically more capable of dealing with the larger stressors in life by first learning how to deal effectively with the smaller, more manageable ones.

Sometimes, the worst part about a stressful experience is anticipating it. Some children worry about getting a less-than-stellar report card. Other children worry about the first day at a new school after moving from another neighborhood. One way to help children manage stress is to teach them how to coach themselves through it, as shown below.

If I am anticipating a stressful experience, then I should tell myself:

- I won't think about how bad I feel; I'll think rationally about what I can do about the situation.

- I have the support and encouragement of people who can help me deal with the problem. I'll call on them if I need to.

- I have already come a long way toward handling the problem; I can go the rest of the way.
- I'll develop a plan to deal with it. That's better than getting upset.
- This could be a rough situation, but I know how to deal with it.
- I'll stick to the issues and not take it personally.
- There won't be any need for an argument. I know what to do.
- As long as I keep my cool, I'm in control of the situation.
- I won't make more out of this than I need to.
- There is no point in getting mad. I will think of what I have to do.
- I'll look for the positives.
- It's probably not so serious.
- My anger is a signal of what I have to do. It's time for problem solving.

To confront and handle the stressor, I should tell myself:
- I can meet this challenge.
- I can do it, one step at a time. I can handle the situation.
- I'll just think about what I have to do.
- This tenseness can be an ally.
- Relax, I'm in control. Take a slow, deep breath.
- There's no need to doubt myself. Focus on the plan.

254 / Stress and Your Child

- There are lots of wonderful things going on in my life; this is only one event.

If I am feeling overwhelmed, I should tell myself:

- Take a deep breath and exhale slowly.

- Focus on what is happening now. What is it I have to do?

- This will be over soon. I can do it.

- I may want to avoid the situation, but I can deal with it.

After a stressful event, I should tell myself:

- It wasn't as bad as I expected.

- I can be pleased with the progress I'm making.

- I did it! I got through it. It was tough, but I did it! Good for me!

- I had a plan and it worked, one step at a time.

Taking a Stressful Experience One Stage at a Time

Every stressful event has a before, a during, and an after. Help your children learn to identify the stages and deal with each one. Go through the following lists with them. Try to give a personal example, unique to your child, for each idea.

Stage One: Before (Preparing for Stress)

You might say: "The worst part about something is anticipating it. We have all been in a situation in which we worried for days about something that had to be done, that we couldn't get out of, that we knew was going to cause us stress. When there is no way to avoid the stressor, the following tips can help."

Review the following guidelines with your child:

1. Stay as calm as possible. Say, "I need to think about what I have to do. I need to use my energy for that."

2. Think of the absolute worst thing that could happen . . . and then remember that the chances of that happening are small. And even if the absolute worst thing does happen, you will still wake up tomorrow morning, the sun will still be shining, and your dog will still lick your face to tell you he loves you.

3. Try not to think about how bad you feel, but rather ask yourself, "What am I going *to do* about it?"

4. Stop making negative statements about yourself. For example, every time you catch yourself saying, "I can't do it," stop and shake your head and say, "I will try my best to do it." Speak positively, not negatively.

5. List all the people you can count on to help you get through it. Say, "I'll have the support and encouragement of family and friends. Even if something awful happens, they'll still be there for me. I can always ask them for help if I need to."

6. Develop a step-by-step plan for getting through the problem. Taking some action, almost any action at all, is better than doing nothing. You need to feel that you have control. Say, "I have handled other problems. I am making progress on this one, too. I'll think about what I have to do; that works better than worrying about it."

Let's take an example: a child's having to give an oral report in front of a class, one of the scariest things that can happen at any age. Go through the steps with your child one by one.

- *Stay as calm as possible.* Picture yourself giving a good speech. Think about your success.

- *Think of the absolute worst that could happen.* Suppose you get tongue-tied and stand up in front of the class and can't get any words out. You stand there for what seems like hours, going, "Uh, uh, uh . . ." The kids are all laughing at you. What can you do? You can laugh along with them. It may be embarrassing, but they all sympathize. They have all gone through the same thing themselves. Your friends might razz you a little bit that day, but by the next day, they'll have forgotten all about it.

- *Develop a step-by-step plan for getting through the problem.* Divide the problem into tiny parts. Maybe the first part is getting your notes ready for the report. Work on them until they are short, clear, and easy to glance at. The next step is getting to the front of the class while everyone is looking at you without stumbling over your own feet. Shift your desk so that you have a clear aisle. Move your backpack away. Sit on the edge of your chair so you can hop up easily. Get everything off your desk so there is no chance of knocking things over when you stand up. Take each step in your mind; visualize yourself going through it. Have a plan for each step along the way.

- *Stop making negative statements about yourself.* If you begin to say, "I can't talk in front of the class—I'll make a fool of myself," take a deep breath and make a new statement. "I will get through this. It's only for a few minutes. I've done it before. I'll have my friends there rooting for me. I can do this."

- *List all the people you can count on to help you get through it.* Your parents will be glad to listen to you practice. Your friends on the telephone can help you rehearse. If you are truly terrified, ask the teacher whether you can come in early or stay late when no one else is in the classroom, so you can stand where you'll have to stand later and go through a trial run. The teacher will understand.

Stage Two: During (When Stress Is Happening to You)
How can you deal with a stressful event while it is happening? Here are some suggestions:

1. Take it one step at a time. Don't overwhelm yourself by trying to rush through it. If you had a chance to make a plan, stick to it. If the stress is sudden and unexpected, deal with it slowly and deliberately. Don't try to do everything at once.

2. Keep focused on what you are doing. It is normal to let concentration wander, to want to be anywhere but where you are when you are stressed. However, if you stay focused on the situation, you can deal with it more efficiently and get through it that much faster.

3. Put the event in perspective. Even if things are going terribly, keep reminding yourself that this is only one little thing in your life. There are a lot of wonderful things you have going for you that will be there long after this is past.

4. Breathe deeply and speak slowly. Even though the adrenaline might be flowing, if you slow down, you will feel more in control, more able to cope. You will let your brain catch up to your body (you probably feel as if your heart is beating a mile a minute!) and see that there are things you can do.

5. Understand that your stress is normal, acceptable. It is nothing to be ashamed of.

6. Focus on the positive. Even though you are totally stressed, you are still functioning. You are still able to talk, to move, to think. You *can* handle the stress that comes along, no matter how severe it may seem to be.

Stage Three: After
Finally, the situation is over. You may be feeling very relieved, but you may also be feeling some of the aftereffects of stress.

1. Congratulate yourself! Say, "I did it! Good for me!"

2. Remind yourself that it wasn't as bad as you expected. Remember all those terrible things you thought might happen? Most of them didn't happen, right? You can laugh about them now.

3. Go back through your plan, if you had one, and see how well it worked. Note the parts that were really good for future reference, and think about the parts that weren't so hot.

Managing Time Wisely

When children are very young, they often complain of being bored. They want their parents' attention at all times and have to be kept busy constantly. But very soon, they outgrow that and go to the other extreme: They are far too busy. Even toddlers have many classes and activities. Older children have full academic class loads at school and are often involved in after-school organizations or sports. They also might do volunteer work or hold down part-time jobs. Then, of course, there is that all-encompassing thing called *a social life*. There are so many things for children to do that it is no wonder they are often overwhelmed. Sometimes they get stressed out when they even *think* about all the things they have to do!

Learning to manage their time wisely and to prioritize what

needs to be done—to do now what needs to be done now, and do next what should be done next—is very important for our children; it helps them feel in control of their lives. By gaining the upper hand on the day, by having a plan of attack, children can lessen those very frightening feelings of not being in charge.

Don't Agonize, Prioritize!

The first step in time management is setting priorities. Ask your children to write down everything they do in a normal week. Encourage them to think of as many things as possible. They may be surprised that the list is shorter (or longer) than they anticipated. Next, break the list into two parts, **A** and **B**. The **A** tasks are the ones that absolutely, positively must be done *now*. The **B** tasks are the things that should be done, but can be done later. Next, each entry on both lists should be weighed. Assign priorities. For example, a teenager's list might look like this:

"A" PRIORITIES (RANKED IN ORDER OF IMPORTANCE)

1. Finish biology assignment
2. Find SAT tutor
3. Buy birthday gift for Mom—today!
4. Meet with coach
5. Clean out locker to find calculator

"B" PRIORITIES

1. Get broken watch repaired
2. Check out books to begin term paper

3. Write Uncle John thank-you letter for birthday cash
4. Start lining up part-time job
5. Schedule an evening to take my sister's turn washing the dishes, as she did for me.

You might also ask your children to write down the names of people whom they could ask for help in completing each task, should they require assistance. For example, if a child needs to finish a paper on the computer he shares with his sister, he might ask her to take over his dog-walking chores for the next few nights to free up more time for him to spend on the computer.

Help your children make out a daily, weekly, and (depending on their age) monthly schedule. Emphasize that these schedules are flexible. The key is to enable your children to see that if they manage time wisely, they can get things done and have time left over for themselves.

Learning to Relax

Relaxing is a key means of reducing stress. When you relax, you become aware of the relationship between your mind and body. You control your breathing, you control your emotions. You calm down. Conscious relaxation makes changes in the electrical activity of the brain, producing feelings of well-being. Relaxation decreases the rate of metabolism and oxygen consumption even more than sleep does.

Children (and adults) are often so wound up that telling them to relax seems futile. They feel that if they were to take the time to relax, they would only be setting their cause further back. Your job is to convince them that a few minutes of relaxation will actually save them time in the long run by making them more productive, more efficient.

Visual Imagery: Relaxing and Rehearsing
There are two basic types of visual imagery: imagery that relaxes, and imagery that rehearses. Used together, these two types of visualization are powerful stress management tools. Your children have probably seen their athletic heroes use visualization techniques. When you watch the Olympics, you see athletes with their eyes shut, swaying back and forth as they go through their routines in their minds. Brian Boitano, the great ice skater, was often shown on television behind the scenes, waiting to get on the ice. He would be bobbing and swaying, shaking his shoulders, moving his arms, going through all the steps and jumps and movements in his mind's eye. This mental preparation removes much of the pressure and lessens stress by making the athletes feel in control.

The same thing can happen for your children. If they go through a visualization in their minds, they will feel they can manage what is going to happen. They will have an idea of the situation that helps chase away the Great Unknown. Go through a visualization exercise yourself a few times before you do one with your children. Learn how to control your thoughts, to use positive ones to block out the negatives. Try the following exercise yourself, then modify it for your children.

Step one: Set the scene. Find a quiet place where you won't be disturbed. You might be able to lock yourself into the bathroom for a nice long bath, or you may have to put a note on your bedroom door that you want twenty minutes of undisturbed time. Lower the lights if possible, to set the mood. Put on some music you find relaxing. (Children might like to get in a favorite chair with headphones.)

Step two: Set a time limit. Allow about fifteen or twenty minutes for this activity. It's important that you be mentally unencumbered; if you try to do this while listening for the baby's cry, or if you feel guilty for spending so much time alone, you won't get into a state of deep relaxation. When you go through this exercise with your children, they might not be able to sit still for more than fifteen minutes. Begin with smaller increments of time (five minutes is a good place to start) and increase it as your child develops his or her ability.

Step three: Let your mind go where it finds peace. Begin by directing your mind to a peaceful place. You may want to visualize yourself walking down the beach on a sunny day. Maybe you like the idea of sailing lazily in a small boat, or lying in a park by a brook. Think of something you have done in the past that was truly wonderful, or something you have always wanted to do. Prepare your mind first. Once you feel relaxed, *then* you can begin the step-by-step visualization of the situation that is truly stressing you now. NOTE: Any time during your visualization that destructive or distressing thoughts begin to intrude, make a conscious effort to block them by going back to the original pleasant scenario. This is not the time to examine troublesome thoughts or feelings.

(When your children do this exercise, talk softly to them

about where they like to be: lying in bed hugging their dog, sitting in the tree house with their best friend. When you see them relax, then talk them slowly through what is bothering them, ending with a positive outcome.)

There is a word-for-word script given in the Appendix of this book. Read it into a cassette recorder (or have someone with a particularly soothing voice read it), then use it when you perform your visualization exercise.

Physical Relaxation: Breathing and Muscle Control

Just as you can learn to relax your mind, you can learn to relax your body. One good way to do so is to practice deep breathing. Very few of us breathe properly. We take shallow breaths, raising and lowering our chests. The best breathing is called "belly breathing" because the stomach expands and contracts. Babies and animals breathe this way naturally; unfortunately, many of us have learned bad habits we need to unlearn now.

As you inhale, the bloodstream is oxygenated and purified. Breathing helps slow down the heartbeat. How many times have your children run in from outside and you have told them, "Slow down, take a deep breath, and then tell me what's happening." Practice deep breathing with your children. Watch them and remind them frequently to practice their breathing. And do so yourself! If your children see you consciously stop and take several deep breaths in a time of stress, they will begin to associate deep breathing with relaxation and emulate you.

Another important type of physical relaxation involves *progressive muscle relaxation*. This is a technique in which each muscle is consciously tightened, held for a few seconds, then released. Try it now. Clench your fists as tightly as possible. Hold for a count of five, then release. Can't you feel how much more relaxed your hands are? Do the same with your shoulders, your calves, your jaw. *There is a word-for-word script for progressive muscle relaxation given in the Appendix of this book.* Again, you can read it into a cassette recorder and then go through it with your children.

Role Playing

Role playing is a skill that allows children to rehearse strategies for resolving a situation. Practicing ahead of time helps the child decide on the best course of action. Here's an example of how role playing was used by Kate and her mother:

Kate's Dilemma
Kate and Alex are best friends. Every Saturday the girls get together around ten o'clock and go to a local shopping mall where young people from a number of schools hang out. There they shop, socialize with their friends, flirt with the boys, have lunch, and sometimes watch a matinee. But Kate has been asked by another friend, Gwen, to go to Gwen's father's cabin on the lake for waterskiing this Saturday. Gwen and Alex don't get along; the invitation doesn't include Alex, only Kate. Kate really wants to go but is worried that she will upset Alex, maybe even getting her so mad that she won't want to be best friends anymore. Kate and her mother go through role playing so she can practice dealing with the problem:

TEST RUN #1

Kate (pretending to phone Alex): Hello, Alex? I'm calling about this Saturday.

Mother (pretending to be Alex): I was just going to call you. Let's wear our denim skirts and our matching red shirts. Oh, by the way, I read that the movie this weekend is the new Kevin Costner one; oooh, he's so cute! And my brother said he can give us a ride this time so we won't have to take the bus. He's going to take me to your place at about ten, then drop us off. Pretty nice of the geek, huh?

Kate: (unprepared for Alex's rush of enthusiasm and not wanting to disappoint her): Uh, uh, oh, okay. Yeah. That's fine. See you at ten. (She slams down the phone.) M-o-o-o-m-m, you're going to have to tell her that I had to go to my cousin's or to see a sick friend or something.

TEST RUN #2

Kate (pretending to phone Alex): Hello, Alex?

Mother (pretending to be Alex): Oh hi, Kate. I can't wait 'til tomorrow because there's a great movie showing—

Kate: Alex, I can't go. I lost a filling and my tooth is killing me. My mom's going to see whether she can get me an emergency dental appointment.

Mother: Oh, okay. I'm sorry. I hope it feels better. Do you want me to come over just to watch TV, or to go to the dentist with you? Just say the word.

Kate: No thanks. I'm so grumpy I don't want to be around anyone. I'll call you Sunday or see you in school Monday.

TEST RUN #3

Kate (pretending to phone Alex): Hi, Alex. I have some bad news.

Mother (pretending to be Alex): What? Don't tell me your mom found out about—

Kate: No, no! No one knows about that but you and me. I just can't make it tomorrow to go to the mall. But maybe on Monday after school we can go and check out those new hats at The Gap.

Mother: But why can't you go?

Kate: Because Gwen asked me to go with her this weekend to her father's cabin on the lake and I said I'd go. I know that you don't really like Gwen, and I know you think she pushes her way into our friendship, but I don't see it that way. You know we're best friends so I'm hoping you won't be upset with my decision to go with her. I wanted to tell you myself and not to lie to you. Are you okay with that, Alex?

Mother: Well, I'm not thrilled, but I guess so. Can we have lunch on Monday, then?

Kate: Absolutely. And let's go to The Gap on Monday after school. Have a good time at the mall if you go, Alex. I'll miss you. See you Monday.

Mother: That won't be easy without my best friend, but I'll try. See you on Monday, Kate. Bye.

Note the role playing has covered three bases. In the first case, Kate never got the chance to cancel her plans because she let Alex make her feel guilty. Instead, she tried to get her mother to take the responsibility for canceling their standing plans. She wasn't prepared. In the second case, Kate out-and-out lied, risking that Alex would somehow find out about Kate's spending the weekend with Gwen and be really upset later. The third scenario found Kate confronting the situation head-on. She also set the stage to broaden her friendships with both girls, and by being assertive in her communication, she did not buy into guilt feelings for making plans that did not include Alex. In addition, she affirmed her friendship with Alex by offering Alex something to look forward to on Monday, softening her disappointment about Saturday.

This role playing can be done in various ways. You and your child can exchange roles, having Kate play Alex and respond the way she thinks Alex would. The goal is to help Kate feel prepared for anything that might arise, even if that something is not pleasant. She might have a little bit of anxiety or guilt or unhappiness over what she does or what the final outcome is, but at least she will have lessened her stress level by playing through the occurrence in advance. By exchanging roles you build confidence in your ability to assert your decision. Such planning reduces the stress in the situation by lowering the risk that you will be overwhelmed at the time of confrontation. It also provides you with an opportunity to assess your child's understanding of the situation and her ability to implement a plan under stress.

Developing Problem-Solving Skills

No one escapes problems. What may seem minor to you, such as not being able to memorize the multiplication tables, can seem the end of the world to your children. Having a problem and not knowing how to remedy it can be frustrating and even debilitating. Sometimes children, especially very young ones, have difficulty identifying and specifying the problem, let alone developing a strategy for solving it. If your children have a plan for solving a problem, they feel much more in control. They know that the problem still exists but feel more confident that they can do something about it. Even if the problem cannot be made to go away entirely, they don't feel so helpless. There is a simple, four-step approach that skilled problem solvers use:

1. Identify the real problem. If your six-year-old son tells you he won't go to school anymore because he hates the teacher, the real problem might be that the teacher is always comparing him to his older siblings who were in her previous classes. If your twelve-year-old daughter tells you she won't play with her best friend Lynda anymore because Lynda is "stupid," the problem may be that Lynda went roller-skating with another friend and didn't invite your daughter. Talk to your children. Have them work backwards from what they are feeling until they can identify what the core problem is.

2. Search for alternative solutions. In the adult world, we call this brainstorming. You have probably gone through an exercise in college or at the office in which a group of people come up with as many solutions to a problem as possible within a given time limit. Some of those solutions are unworkable, some are truly bizarre, but the point is to come up with as many as you can. Your child can do the same. Have him or her think of many solutions, including funny ones (laughing at a problem is a great way of reducing its stressful effect). Help your children by reminding them of parallel situations you or they were in, or situations they have read about or seen on television or heard about from their friends.

3. Evaluate the possible consequences. Every action has a reaction. Any time a step is taken to solve a problem, there will be consequences. For example, if the problem is that Brent doesn't want to be friends with Jeremy anymore, the consequences might be that Jeremy's other friends will drop Brent. Have your child identify the possible consequences and decide whether he or she can live with them.

4. Choose a solution and develop a plan. After your child has come up with several solutions, he or she should narrow them down to a few and then finally choose one. After that solution has been chosen, develop a plan to implement it. For example, if the solution to not having enough money to buy the latest fashions is to take a part-time job, sit down and write out a list of stores or other places to which your children could apply for jobs. If the problem is that your daughter is bored because her best friend is away for the summer, the solution might be to get her involved in a youth group. List several youth groups and have her call the supervisors of each to select the one that sounds like the most fun.

Davis's Story
Here's an exercise in problem solving you can do with your children:

Nine-year-old Davis is always late for class. Yesterday the teacher sent home a note saying that for the fourth time in only two weeks, Davis ran into the classroom more than five minutes after the bell had sounded. Since Davis lives only a ten-minute walk from school and always leaves home in plenty of time to get there, he has no legitimate reason for being late. His mother thinks about punishing Davis but decides to hone his problem-solving skills instead.

1. Identify the real problem. To his mother, the problem is that Davis is late for school. She sits down and discusses it with him. She hears that he leaves home in plenty of time and arrives on the school grounds in time, but then he always goes over to his friend Martin's classroom to copy his homework before the bell rings. They talk until the last minute, then Davis has to run for his class and is usually late. He is so worried about being caught running down the halls by the principal that he takes the long way to his classroom, going around the outside of the whole school to avoid going past the principal's office. This makes Davis quite late.

The real problem in this case obviously is not Davis's being late but his not getting his homework done the night before. He tells his mother that sometimes he gets it done but is not sure that he has the right answers and needs to check with Martin, who always gets his homework right. There are two problems: lack of time management (most nights, Davis watches TV instead of doing his homework) and low self-esteem (needing to have his work verified by someone else).

2. Search for alternative solutions. Davis and his mother decide to focus on the problem of poor time management. They write up a list of alternative solutions that include the following:

- no TV until all homework is done
- schedule time to talk with Martin every night on the telephone
- discuss homework with parents right after dinner
- stay after school for the half-hour study hall that is offered and do homework then
- get up earlier in the morning and do homework before breakfast
- stop doing homework (Guess whose suggestion this one was?)

3. Evaluate the possible consequences. Most of the consequences look great. Davis will be doing his homework himself rather than copying someone else's work. He will learn more and feel better about himself. By having a regular time to talk with his friend Martin, he'll be able to double-check his work and feel comfortable that it's right.

4. Choose a solution and develop a plan. Davis and his mother decide to select two of the ideas and combine them. First, Davis is going to enroll in the after-school study hall that the school offers. In that half hour, he should be able to get almost all of his homework done. Davis usually comes home and watches TV, but "since there's nothing good on at that time anyway," he doesn't mind staying after school.

Second, Davis is going to try to schedule a time with Martin to talk on the phone for about ten minutes every night, just enough time to check over the answers, but not enough time to get them from Martin and write them all down. (Davis himself came up with the idea that he should be the one to read the answers to Martin, rather than having Martin read them to Davis. "That way I'll have to do the work, and Martin can just tell me if I'm wrong.") They will have the same telephone time each night, and Davis's siblings will be told they can't be on the telephone at that time. This double-checking will ensure that Davis feels confident about his work.

Appreciating Family Relationships

When family relationships break down, they produce a good share of the pain and stress we feel. Conversely, when our relations with family members are rich and nourishing, they can be a potent source of good feelings that contribute to our sound emotional health. Because family members are anchors in both good and bad times, they help buffer outside forces of stress by making that stress seem less significant.

When our children know how to sustain dynamic and fruitful relationships at home and can recognize the important role those relationships play in their lives, they will be better able to see how the family serves as a stress buffer. The following exercise is to help your children see who is there for them when they need help, and how the help from that person goes a long way toward reducing stress.

To introduce this exercise you might say, "Often other people—family members and other people besides family members—believe in us and help us cope with stressful and painful times. Sometimes young people underestimate how extensive their base of people who support and root for them really is.

Who lifts your spirits when you are down and helps you reduce stress by showing support? What kind of support does this person give you?" Let's see how Tony responded.

Tony's Family
Several members of Tony's family are willing to help him when he has a problem.

Who: "My Mom."
How she serves as a stress buffer: "Last week I had to give a book report in front of my class and I was really nervous. That morning my mother fixed me a special breakfast, practiced my report with me, and put a 'You can do it! I love you!' note in my lunch."

Who: "My stepdad."
How he serves as a stress buffer: "Yesterday, when I forgot my lunch money, my dad brought me some even though he had to leave work and drive to school. He wasn't angry, and he didn't lecture me about being forgetful. He wanted me to be able to have lunch."

Who: "My dog, Kukabear."
How she serves as a stress buffer: "My puppy is loyal to me, coming and following when I call her. When I am sad, my puppy senses my sadness and cuddles in my lap."

Who: "My big brother Ron."
How he serves as a stress buffer: "When no other kids ask me to sit with them in the lunchroom, he does. Even though

he teases me, when he hears other kids tease me he comes to my defense."

Tapping into the Power of Friendships

Friendship is one of the best stress-busters around. Good friends provide support, advice, and comfort during stressful times. Your friends are there to listen to you when you are unhappy or worried. They have seen you at your best and your worst and are still friends with you. They provide a lot of support; you know you can go to them with problems. Having that support, advice, and comfort can get you through some pretty stressful times.

Talk to your children about true friends. You might say, "Take advantage of the power that friendship offers. Be sure to develop positive friendships with cheerful, happy, positive people. Don't get close to those who are negative and gloomy, always whining and complaining. (And remember that most people are attracted to people just like them. If you're a Gloomy Gus, your friends will be the whiny kind. But if you make an effort to be upbeat and look for the good side of things, happy people will be attracted to you.) Think about the people who are your friends and how much they help you cope with stress. Even friends who are not there every day for you, like an old buddy you had to leave behind when you moved, are important sources of support."

Help your child identify the friendships he or she has by asking the following questions. Just as you can cheer up by counting your blessings when things go wrong, you can feel stronger by counting your friends when you don't think you can handle things yourself.

1. Who is always willing to listen to me?
2. Who makes me laugh?
3. Whom can I confide in?
4. Who gives me tactful, useful feedback?
5. Who have I met who might become a good friend?

Using Your Sense of Humor

There's one skill we all have for fighting stress that we tend to underestimate: our sense of humor. A sense of humor can be a real asset in times of stress. Eleventh-grader Marilee went to the school dance with her date, who was in his Army ROTC uniform. She was escorted up to the stage by him, where she was supposed to introduce a community leader. She had on a bracelet with a clasp that got entangled in her date's sleeve. It seemed as if everyone was looking at the two as she struggled to free herself. Finally, she looked up, smiled at everyone, and said with a laugh, "Well, Mother always told me to snag an Army man!" Everyone laughed, and the tension lifted.

Humor provides both comic relief and a moment of distance from problems. Even desperately ill people look for the humor in their situations. Humor is one way to alleviate feelings of terror and helplessness. Obviously it's not okay to make jokes at other people's expense, but it is okay to laugh at frightening situations (remember Joan Rivers's *Having a Baby Can Be a Scream?*). We all have a sense of humor; some of us just haven't given it much exercise lately. We can bring it to the forefront by consciously trying to see the humor in the little things that happen every day.

Here is a fun exercise to do with your children. Begin by

thinking about the most stressful incident of the week. Now consider it in a humorous light. What would Billy Crystal or Whoopi Goldberg or the guys from *Wayne's World* say about that moment? They would probably crack a joke. Now, you may say that you can't think of jokes that quickly, but even a simple laugh can make everyone forget the problem and focus on your good humor. Laughter is probably the most contagious and best thing you have to spread.

Tell your children that they can "prepare" humor by having a few funny stories to drag out if they need to. For example, whenever Lael feels that she is pushed to the limit, she tells of the time that her four-year-old brother went running naked into the middle of one of her slumber parties, grabbed a candy bar from the hand of one of the girls at the party, slipped, and landed in the living room with the dog on top of him barking madly and lapping at the chocolate. Lael practiced telling the story until she could do it well, with good gestures and funny voices.

It is important to see the funny side of things that happen to you personally. It's best to convey this to your child before he or she has a stressful experience, not after he or she is in tears. Try to think of examples. For instance, you might say to your child, "If your pants split up the middle when you are bending over to get the Jello in the cafeteria line, of course you will be embarrassed. But why not laugh along with the others? You couldn't feel any worse; laughing is bound to make you feel better. It will also make the others remember your laughing more than your underwear, something you will appreciate later."

Try the following exercise with your children:

1. Try to remember one totally embarrassing thing that happened to you each year since you've been five. You probably can't, right? That's because you forget the bad times. Now try to remember something funny that happened to you each year. Chances are, you have several good stories. Humor is much more memorable than embarrassment.

2. Describe a time when a friend was under a lot of stress but managed to laugh about her situation. Maybe your friend was going to get her tonsils out but giggled about how her throat would swell up and make her look like a bullfrog. Remember how she not only felt better but made you feel better as well? Neither of you was quite as afraid when you kept giggling over how she would look all puffed up.

3. Think of the stressor you are dealing with now. Can you find anything to laugh about in the situation? For example, maybe the most nerve-racking thing to you is asking someone out on a date. Can you picture yourself telling your grandchildren fifty years from now how silly you were, hemming and hawing? Pretend you are someone else observing the situation. Can't you see something funny there?

4. Always remember that most good comedians take their material from their own lives. It's the silly little things that happen to all of us that make the best jokes and stories. When you can laugh at yourself, you relieve stress and get some good material for your next talk with your best friend, all at the same time!

Monitoring Nutrition and Diet

Prolonged stress puts a major physical strain on the body, using up essential minerals and vitamins, depleting the body of the nutrients it needs to run efficiently. Diet can profoundly affect emotional stability and adaptability to stress, and certain foods can alter our state of mind in much the same way as alcohol and drugs. Think of the food that is going into today's children. Over 50 percent of the average American's diet consists of processed food. In our foods can be found more than four thousand additives, few of which have been thoroughly tested for their effects on our central nervous systems. We have become a nation of fast-food junkies, cola drinkers, and refined-carbohydrate fanatics.

Diet affects emotional balance. Like the rest of the body, brain cells require proper feeding in order to function correctly. The brain is the body's most chemically sensitive organ. Deprived of proper nutrients or overwhelmed by pollutants, it performs poorly. There was an interesting study conducted by the San Luis Obispo Juvenile Probation Department in California several years ago. Difficult juvenile offenders were tested and found to have severe imbalances in their body chemistry. Their typical diets consisted of no breakfast, excessive nighttime eating, refined-carbohydrate snacks, and heavy consumption in general of junk food containing sugar, salt, and caffeine. These children, when stressed, exhibited anxiety, blurred vision, depression, insomnia, nightmares, muscle aches, joint pain, dizziness and faintness, and a craving for alcohol and sweets.

A good diet is more than just a good idea; it is essential for helping your children cope with stress. When their bodies are functioning at peak efficiency, they are better able to put stressors in proper perspective, less likely to fly off the handle and overreact to them. Children who have good nutrition have more ammunition to fight the stressors, can fight them longer before becoming burned out, and are able to spring back to normal more quickly when they do become exhausted. While you probably know the basics of a good diet, take a few minutes to review the following suggestions. Remember: Your children's physical health goes a long way toward determining their mental and emotional health.

- Provide adequate protein. To calculate the number of grams of protein your child needs, divide his body weight by two. For example, a hundred-pound child needs 50 grams of protein daily. This protein can be animal (meat) or vegetable.

- Supply whole grains rather than more highly refined and processed foods, including bread and cereal.

- Make fruits and nuts available for snacking, rather than junk food.

- Offer a good breakfast and a sparing dinner. Three well-balanced meals a day are vital. Some children (especially teenagers) eat more than three a day; the number is not as important as the nutritional balance.

- Avoid using junk food as a reward; giving candy bars before bedtime for completing a homework assignment sends the wrong message.

• Try to keep out of your house—or at least away from your children—processed or packaged food, sugar, white bread, white flour, cakes, and alcohol.

• Be on the lookout for "hidden" junk food, including canned fruits and flavored yogurt, which can have a high sugar content.

Talk to Your Children about the Diet-Stress Connection
Since no parent can monitor her children's eating habits all the time, it is important that your children have some self-discipline. Talk to your children about the connection between what goes into their bodies and how they feel and react. Give them examples: "Do you remember, Alison, how nervous you were before that big test? You didn't eat breakfast and then complained of a headache and a sick stomach. Then you had a soda and candy bar at school and said you were so jittery you didn't do too well. The caffeine in your soda and candy probably made you even more nervous than you already were. You can't do that if you want to think clearly and have your body perform efficiently." When your son had a particularly good day, made a touchdown, scored well on a test, go back and identify what foods he consumed that day or in the previous few days. Talk to him about how his good diet made his day go well. Do the same in reverse when things are going badly. You might even encourage your children to keep a journal of what they eat and how they react to stress. The key is to make them aware of their eating habits so that they improve their nutrition away from home while you are improving it at home.

Increasing Exercise

One of the best things anyone can do to relieve stress is to relieve the physical tension. When you run around and whack a tennis ball, you get rid of a lot of aggressions that tighten up your shoulders and make you feel tense and stiff. When you are feeling stressed out, exercise will give your mind something else to focus on. You can give yourself a natural high by doing enjoyable activities that provide exercise: basketball, touch football, volleyball, biking, tennis. Children can just run around. Anything you can do that requires movement and energy works off a lot of your stress and pressure.

When you watch your children run around the house, you probably envy them their energy and think that the last thing they need is more exercise. However, the statistics don't agree. The U.S. Department of Health and Human Services issued a report in 1990 saying that 80 to 90 percent of Americans fail to get enough exercise. Many of these are children, who sit and watch TV or play video games rather than go outside and play. A generation ago children walked to school or rode their bikes there. Today, children are bused to schools too far to walk to. Even kids in neighborhood schools may be driven to school because of parental fears—not unjustified—about the crazies who could accost the children on their way to school.

Schools don't provide as much exercise within the classroom as they used to. Budget constraints have forced cutbacks in physical education classes. Children might have one class a week. For older children, the school district can save the cost of towel service and water for the showers. Enrollment in physical education classes used to be mandatory. Now some districts allow children to take a written exam based on a textbook and get credit for the class. No more changing into shorts and a T-shirt and going out there and getting all hot and sweaty.

There is no doubt that exercise helps children deal with stress. It provides the following benefits, which have been discussed elsewhere in this book as well:

- increases circulation

- assists the heart

- adds oxygen to the body

- aids digestion

- relaxes nerves, balances emotions

- increases resistance to disease

- reduces fatigue

- strengthens muscles, bones, and ligaments

- improves figure and complexion

- sharpens mental powers

Making Exercise a Family Priority
Since exercise is so vital to stress reduction, and since we can't count on the schools to provide it, we as parents need to make exercise one of our top priorities. You can take an active role in getting your children out of the house and into physical fitness.

1. Set an example. "Do as I say, not as I do" doesn't work with children who ask why you are making them ride their bikes to school when you hop into the car to go two blocks to the 7-Eleven. As a role model, you need to show your children that exercise is a vital part of your life, that you recognize its importance. Along with showing this, don't be afraid to say something. When you come back from a wearying day, you might say, "I'm tempted just to plop on the couch and vegetate. But I know that I'll feel worse if I do that. If I go take a long walk, I'll feel better and get more sleep tonight. Here I go, lazybones and all." When your exercise has given you a high, tell your children why you are so cheerful and peppy.

2. Develop family fitness. Time together is at a premium in most families. A good way to spend it is exercising. Ride your bikes together. Take walks together. Go Rollerblading or ice-skating together. Take a swim in the lake together. No matter how young or old your children, you can find some family activity that will be fun for them and will get them—and you—in shape at the same time. Make these fitness routines a part of your daily or weekly schedule. Plan time to go to the park, just as you would schedule time to go see a school play or to go to the movies. If you take work home with you from the office, getting out and exercising can make a big difference in how refreshed you are when you go back to that bulging briefcase.

3. Follow the *Reader's Digest* suggestions for family fitness. *Reader's Digest* magazine has four suggestions for working on family fitness. These are:

- *Commit to a contract.* Draw up a contract for each member of the family, saying what he is going to do, what goals he is working toward. For example, maybe your ten-year-old's goal is to be able to jog one mile by the end of the month. Put that in writing. Have the child sign and date the contract, and have another family member sign it as a witness.

- *Exercise as a family.* As noted earlier, this is a way to spend time together. It is also an excellent way to motivate each other. It doesn't have to be a major undertaking. Just walking around the yard or up and down the street for a half hour before dinner will suffice. The important thing is to get out and do something, anything. It doesn't have to involve driving long distances to a court or a gym or buying expensive equipment.

- *Keep records.* Children love to see how they progress. If appropriate for your children, post a chart on the refrigerator showing how many goals they have reached. Update the chart regularly.

- *Reward achievements.* When your children accomplish something that increases their fitness, or when they meet a goal, reward them. Don't sabotage your efforts by giving them a candy reward; make it something like fitness clothing or sports equipment. When the whole family reaches a major goal, you might reward yourselves with a

fitness vacation. Go backpacking in a national
park or canoeing down a river.

Keep track of how much better you handle stress because of
exercise. No doubt you will find that stressors seem less numerous and less severe. For example, a child who used to worry
and cry a lot over homework that never seemed to get done may
have more endurance now and be able to work harder and accomplish more. Point out the way exercise helps to reduce
stress.

Afterword

By now you are well aware that helping your children learn to manage stress is not a simple task. It takes time, practice, and dedication from you as well as from your children. But it's well worth it. The skills your children learn in their childhood years not only enable them to manage the stress and strains that are sure to be a part of their lives as they go about learning and growing, adapting and changing, but will have payoffs for them later in life as well. Helping your children learn skills to manage stress arms them with a powerful tool—useful in a world where urgency and complexity are going to define their lives.

We want our children to succeed and not to fail. Children who are able to put stress into perspective, who know appropriate and useful skills to reduce it and draw vitality from it, are those who succeed. Over the years, I have watched children succeed and have seen children fail. It's surprising how fine the line is between the two. Many children who do not succeed in school lack the skills to manage the stress, strains, and pressures of being a student.

You can help *your* child succeed in life. By teaching your child ways to effectively manage himself in stressful encounters, you give your child one of the most important skills he will ever learn.

Appendix

Progressive Muscle Relaxation: A Word-by-Word Script

Progressive muscle relaxation is a technique in which each muscle is consciously tightened, held for a few moments, then released.

To begin, find a quiet place where you won't be disturbed. Lower the lights if possible, to set the mood. Put on some music you find relaxing. (Children might like to get in a favorite chair with headphones.) Allow about fifteen or twenty minutes for this activity. When you go through this exercise with your children, they might not be able to sit still for more than fifteen minutes. Begin with shorter sessions and increase their length as your child develops his or her ability.

For Total Body Tension

First, tense every muscle in your body. Tense the muscles of your jaw, eyes, arms, hands, chest, back, stomach, legs, and feet. Feel the tension all over your body. . . . Hold the tension briefly, then relax and let go as you breathe out. . . . Let your whole body relax. . . . Feel a wave of calm come over you as you stop tensing.

Take another deep breath. . . . Study the tension as you hold your breath. . . . Slowly breathe out and relax and let go. Feel the deepening relaxation. Allow yourself to drift more and more with this relaxation. . . . As you continue, you will exercise different parts of your body. Become aware of your body and its tension and relaxation. This will help you become deeply relaxed.

Head and Face

Keeping the rest of your body relaxed, wrinkle your forehead. Do you feel the tension? Your forehead is very tight. Briefly pause and be aware of it. . . . Now relax and let go. Feel the tension slipping out. Smooth out your forehead and take a deep breath. Hold it briefly. Breathe out and relax.

Squint your eyes. Keep the rest of your body relaxed. Briefly pause and feel the tension around your eyes. Take a deep breath and hold it. Breathe out and relax.

Open your mouth as wide as you can. Feel the tension in your jaw and chin. Briefly hold the tension. Now let your mouth gently close. As you do, silently say, "Relax and let go." Take a deep breath. Hold it. As you breathe out, relax and let go.

Close your mouth. Push your tongue against the roof of your mouth. Study the tension in your mouth and chin. Briefly hold the tension. . . . Relax. Take a deep breath. Hold it. Now relax and let go as you breathe out. When you breathe out, let your tongue rest comfortably in your mouth, and let your lips be slightly apart.

Keep the rest of your body relaxed but clench your jaw tightly. Feel the tension in your jaw muscles. Briefly hold the tension. . . . Now relax and let go. Take a deep breath. Hold it. Again, relax and let go as you breathe out.

Think about the top of your head, your forehead, eyes, jaws, and cheeks. Make sure these muscles are relaxed. . . . Have you let go of all the tension? Continue to let the tension slip away and feel the relaxation replace the tension. Feel your face becoming very smooth and soft as all the tension slips away. . . . Your eyes are relaxed. . . . Your tongue is relaxed. Your jaws are loose and limp. . . . All of your neck muscles are also very, very relaxed.

All of the muscles of your face and head are relaxing more and more. . . . Your head feels as though it could roll from side to side.

Shoulders
Now shrug your shoulders up and try to touch your ears with your shoulders. Feel the tension in the shoulders and neck. Hold the tension—now relax and let go. Take a deep breath. Hold it. Relax and let go as you slowly breathe out.

Notice the difference as the tension gives way to relaxation. Shrug your right shoulder up and try to touch your right ear. Feel the tension in your right shoulder and along the left side of your neck. Hold the tension—now relax and let go. Take a deep breath. Hold it. Relax and let go as you slowly breathe out.

Next, shrug your left shoulder up and try to touch your left ear. Feel the tension in your left shoulder and along the right side of your neck. Hold the tension—now relax and let go. Take a deep breath. Hold it. Relax and let go as you slowly breathe out. Feel the relax-

ation seeping into your shoulders. As you continue, you will become loose, limp, and as relaxed as sand.

Arms and Hands

Stretch your arms out and make your hands into fists. Feel the tension in your hands and forearms. Hold the tension. Hold, then relax and let go. Take a deep breath. Hold it. Relax and let go as you slowly breathe out.

Push your right hand down into the surface it is resting on. Feel the tension in your arm and shoulder. Hold the tension—now relax and let go. Take a deep breath. Hold it. Relax and let go as you slowly breathe out.

Next, push your left hand down into whatever it is resting on. Feel the tension in your arm and shoulder. Hold the tension—now relax and let go. Take a deep breath. Hold it. Relax and let go as you slowly breathe out.

Bend your arms toward your shoulders and double them up as if you were showing off your muscles. Feel the tension. Hold the tension. . . . now relax and let go. Take a deep breath. Hold it. Relax and let go as you slowly breathe out.

Chest and Lungs

Move on to the relaxation of your chest. Begin by taking a deep breath that totally fills your lungs. As you hold your breath, notice the tension. Be aware of the tension around your ribs. . . . Relax and let go as you slowly breathe out. Feel the deepening relaxation as you continue breathing easily, freely, and gently.

Take another deep breath. Hold it and again feel the contrast between tension and relaxation. As you do, tighten your chest muscles.

Hold the tension. Relax and let go as you slowly breathe out. Feel the relief as you breathe out and continue to breathe gently. Breathe as smoothly as you can. You will become more and more relaxed with every breath.

Back

Keep your face, neck, arms, and chest as relaxed as possible. Arch your back up (or forward, if you are sitting). Arch it as though you had a pillow under the middle and lower parts of your back. Observe the tension along both sides of your back. Briefly hold that position. Now relax and let go. Take a deep breath. Hold it. Relax and let go as you breathe out. Let that relaxation spread deep into your shoulders and down into your back muscles.

Feel the slow relaxation developing and spreading all over. Feel it going deeper and deeper. Allow your entire body to relax. Face and head relaxed . . . neck relaxed . . . shoulders relaxed . . . arms relaxed . . . chest relaxed . . . back relaxed. . . . All these areas are relaxing more and more, becoming more deeply relaxed.

Stomach

Now begin the relaxation of the stomach area. Tighten up this area. Briefly hold the tension. . . . Relax and let go. Feel the relaxation pour into your stomach area. All the tension is being replaced with relaxation. Take a deep breath. Hold it. Relax and let go as you slowly breathe out.

Now experience a different type of tension in the stomach area. Push your stomach out as far as you can. Briefly hold the tension. . . . Now relax and let go. Take a deep breath. Hold it. Relax and let go as you slowly breathe out. Now pull your stomach in. Imagine pulling your stomach in until it touches your backbone. Hold it. . . . Now relax and let go. Take a deep breath. Hold it. Relax and let go as you breathe out.

You are becoming more and more relaxed. Each time you breathe out, feel the gentle relaxation in your lungs and in your body.

Hips, Legs, and Feet

Begin the relaxation of your hips and legs. Tighten your hips and legs by pressing down the heels of your feet into the surface they are resting on. Tighten these muscles. Keep the rest of your body as relaxed as you can and press your heels down. . . . Now hold the tension. . . . Relax and let go. Your legs feel as if they could float up. Take a deep breath. Hold it. Relax and let go as you slowly breathe out. Feel the relaxation pouring in.

Next, tighten your lower leg muscles. Feel the tension. Briefly hold the tension. . . . Now relax and let go. Take a deep breath. Hold it. Relax and let go as you breathe out.

Now curl your toes downward. Curl them down and try to touch the bottoms of your feet with your toes. Hold them and feel the tension. . . . Relax and let go. Wiggle your toes gently as you let go of the tension. Take a deep breath. Hold it. Relax and let go as you breathe out.

Bend your toes up toward your knees. Feel the tension. Imagine touching your knees with your toes. Feel the tension. Hold the tension. . . . Relax and let go. Feel all the tension vanish. Take a deep breath. Hold it. Relax and let go as you slowly breathe out. Feel the tension leaving your body and the relaxation seeping in.

You have progressed through all the major muscles of your body. Notice the difference between tension and relaxation. Now let your muscles become more and more relaxed. Continue to feel yourself becoming more and more relaxed each time you breathe out. Your whole body is becoming more and more relaxed with each breath. Enjoy the relaxation.

Spend a few more minutes relaxing if you like. If you find yourself getting upset about something later on, remember the relaxation you have just experienced. Before getting upset, take a deep breath, hold it, and as you slowly breathe out silently say, "Relax and let go." With practice, you will be able to use this technique to relax whenever you begin to feel stress.

It is important to include an ending process at the end of the relaxation exercise. This process consists of flexing the arms, taking a deep breath, and slowly opening the eyes. This helps the system adjust gradually to the higher state of arousal needed for getting up and walking around. You might say in the script, *"Now flex your arms. Take a deep breath and release it slowly. I'm now going to count from four to one. When I reach one, your eyes will open and you will be awake, feeling calm and comfortable. Four . . . three . . . two . . . one. Open your eyes, feeling calm and comfortable."* (The count is done slowly, allowing the relaxation period to end easily and quietly. Since the relaxation state is similar to a sleep state, the final steps allow a better transition to alertness.)

Use this or one of the following relaxation techniques at least three times each week, more often if possible, especially at those times when you recognize that you need to lower your stress level—for instance, to calm down before going to bed on an evening when you are feeling particularly excited or keyed up.

Notice how you feel afterward. During the first two weeks of practicing this skill, check for physical signs indicating that you are tense. To look for cues that your body is tensing up, ask yourself these questions:

- Is my forehead wrinkled?
- Are my jaw muscles tight?
- Is my stomach knotted up?
- Are my fists clenched?

Use relaxation ,to replace tension. Tensing and relaxing muscles can help you increase your awareness of your body's muscular response to stress. As you become more aware of the location and feeling of muscle tension, the absence of tension becomes clearer.

Mental Relaxation (Visual Imagery) Exercise

It is possible to relax your mind as well as your body, and it's just as important. *Visual imagery*, sometimes called guided imagery or visualization, is a powerful tool in relaxation. The goal of imagery is to reduce and control mental anxiety. Visual imagery is a technique to produce positive, relaxing images and thoughts that can be used to block out intruding and upsetting ones. You can learn how to do this with imagery training. For example, you may be physically tired but unable to sleep because of upsetting thoughts. By using pleasant visual images, you can control upsetting thoughts and enjoy a deep state of relaxation. To control your thoughts, you need to know what thoughts soothe you, practice summoning those thoughts, and then use them when you want to relax.

Mental imagery is a little like a daydream. You may want to start by trying to visualize a pleasant scene, perhaps one you have seen many times. Try to reexperience the scene in every way you can, with other sensory images such as smell (for example, the scent of flowers), touch (the feel of the grass beneath your feet), hearing (the sound of birds singing in the trees), and taste (the salt air at the beach). Soothing music can also be used to achieve a calm state. When you practice visual imagery using a taped script, you may want to add your favorite calming music to the recording.

To get used to this technique, begin with exercises that proceed from simple images to more complex ones. The steps are outlined below. Once you're able to visualize freely, begin to create your own images. Only you can know what images are relaxing to you. Be patient with yourself as you begin to learn mental relaxation. Complete concentration, even on pleasant images, requires a great deal of practice. Don't get upset if unwanted thoughts come to your mind. Simply redirect your thoughts.

To prepare, find a quiet place without distractions. Sit or lie down. Get comfortable. Loosen any tight-fitting clothing.

1. Close your eyes.

2. Relax your muscles. You may use breathing or muscle-relaxation exercises to become relaxed.

3. Take a deep breath. Imagine breathing in the clean air. As you breathe out, feel the relaxation spread over your body. As you take another breath, feel yourself floating down.

4. Tense and relax your muscles.

5. Imagine or picture yourself doing something relaxing. Get the full picture in your mind.

6. When you are finished, stretch your arms, take a deep breath, and open your eyes.

Here are some ideas for guiding visual imagery:

You are lying on the beach under the warm sun. The sand feels nice and soft underneath you. You're very calm and relaxed, almost falling asleep. The ocean breeze feels good against your skin. You can taste the salt air on your lips. You can hear the waves rolling in gently. You feel very comfortable, relaxed, peaceful, and calm . . .

You are walking slowly through a beautiful green forest. The only sounds you can hear are the songs of the birds and the rush of water flowing over a waterfall in the distance. It is very peaceful, and you continue to walk slowly and quietly, enjoying the calm and peace. It is a warm day, but the forest is very comfortable. You have the forest all to yourself with nothing to disturb you. You begin to hum your favorite tune . . .

It is a lazy Saturday morning. Everyone else is still asleep. A cool rain is falling outside, making gentle sounds that can be heard against your window. You are still sleepy. The fluffy covers on your bed are warm and soft. You bask in the thought of not having to get up, and you turn over and begin to daydream about something you like . . .

Creating Your Own Visualization
Using your imagination, create your own relaxing picture.

1. Name a place that makes you feel relaxed._____

2. Put yourself in a beautiful and serene setting. What are you doing?_____

3. What's the weather like there?_____

4. How do you feel when you are there?_____

5. Why would you like to return?_____

While learning this technique, practice it two or three times each week. Make a point of taking time out for visual imagery relaxation, and describe how you feel afterward: "That is a fantastic feeling. I really feel mentally calm now." Visual imagery can be used for tasks other than relaxing. As you visualize yourself in conflict or in a problem situation, try to imagine yourself dealing successfully with it. When you select your thoughts, you have a better chance to be in charge of your emotions and are more likely to be in control of your behavior.

The Holmes–Rahe Social Readjustment Rating Scale

D r. Thomas H. Holmes, a psychiatrist at the University of Washington School of Medicine, and Dr. Richard H. Rahe constructed a scale of stress values measured in "life change units" (LCU). Stress scores are attached to specific life events. Put a check mark next to each event that has occurred in your life within the past year. When you are finished, add up your LCU score. According to Holmes and Rahe, a score of 150 or less indicates a 35 percent chance a person will get sick or have an accident within the next two years; a score of 150–300 means the chance of an accident or illness within the next two years is 51 percent; a score over 300 means the chance is 80 percent.

THE HOLMES-RAHE SCALE	LCU VALUE
1. Death of a spouse	100
2. Divorce	73
3. Marital separation	65
4. Detention in jail or other institution	63
5. Death of a close family member	63
6. Major personal injury or illness	53
7. Marriage	50
8. Being fired at work	47
9. Marital reconciliation	45
10. Retirement from work	45
11. Major change in the health or behavior of a family member	44
12. Pregnancy	40
13. Sexual difficulty	40
14. Gaining a new family member through birth, adoption, or remarriage	39
15. Major business readjustment	39
16. Major change in financial state	38
17. Death of a close friend	37
18. Change to a different line of work	36
19. Major increase in the number of arguments with spouse	35
20. Taking on a mortgage (purchasing home, business)	31
21. Foreclosure on a mortgage or loan	30
22. Major change in responsibilities at work (promotion, demotion, transfer)	29
23. Son or daughter leaving home	29
24. In-law troubles	29

25. Outstanding personal achievement   28
26. Spouse beginning or ceasing work outside the
    home   26
27. Going back to school   26
28. Major change in living condition (building a new
    home, remodeling, deterioration of home)   25
29. Revision of personal habits   24
30. Troubles with supervisor, boss, superiors   23
31. Major changes in working hours or conditions   20
32. Change in residence   20
33. Change to a new school   20
34. Major change in usual type and/or amount of
    recreation   19
35. Major change in church activities   19
36. Major change in social activities   18
37. Purchasing a car, or other big purchases   17
38. Major change in sleeping habits   16
39. Major change in number of family get-togethers   15
40. Major change in eating habits   15
41. Vacation   13
42. Christmas or holiday observances   12
43. Minor violations of the law (traffic tickets)   11

Suggested Readings

Bettancourt, J. *Am I Normal?* New York: Avon, 1983.

Bingham, E. Edmondson, and S. J. Stryker. *Choices: A Teen Man's Journal for Self-Awareness and Personal Planning.* Mission Publications, El Toro, CA.

———. *Choices: A Teen Woman's Journal for Self-Awareness and Personal Planning.* Mission Publications, El Toro, CA.

Blume, J. *Are You There, God? It's Me, Margaret.* New York: Dell, 1970.

———. *Then Again, Maybe I Won't.* New York: Dell, 1971.

Bradley, B. *Where Do I Belong? A Kid's Guide to Stepfamilies.* Reading, Mass.: Addison-Wesley, 1982.

Brophy, Beth. "Children Under Stress." *U.S. News & World Report* (October 27, 1986): 58–63.

Creighton, Linda. "Kids Taking Care of Kids." *U.S. News & World Report* (December 20, 1993): 26–34.

Danziger, P. *The Cat Ate My Gymsuit.* New York: Dell, 1973.

Dryden, Gordon, and Jeannette Vos. *The Learning Revolution.* Rolling Hills Estates, Calif.: Jalmar Press, 1994.

Duffy, Michael, and Nancy Traver-Washington. "Suffer the Little Children." *Time* (October 8, 1990): 40–50.

"Family Fitness: A Complete Exercise Program for Ages Six to Sixty-Plus." *Reader's Digest* (special report, 1989): 2–12.

Gardner, R. *The Boys and Girls Book about StepFamilies.* New York: Bantam, 1982.

"Has Rock Gone Too Far?" *People* (September 16, 1985): 47–53.

Holmes, T. H., and R. H. Rahe. "The Social Readjustment Rating Scale." *Journal of Psychosomatic Research.* 11 (1967): 213–218.

Johnson, Constance. "Violence in the Schools." *U.S. News & World Report* (November 8, 1993): 31–47.

Kohn, Alfie. "Making The Most of Marriage." *Psychology Today* (December 1987): 9–8.

Krantzler, Mel. *Creative Marriage.* New York: McGraw-Hill, 1981.

LeShan, E. *What's Going to Happen to Me? When Parents Separate or Divorce.* New York: Four Winds Press, 1978.

Morrow, Lance. "Growing Up in America: Through the Eyes of Children." *Time* (August 8, 1988): 31–57.

Pelletier, K. *Mind as Healer, Mind as Slayer.* New York: Delacorte, 1977.

Ripple, Richard E., Robert R. Biehler, and Gail A. Jaquish. *Human Development.* Boston: Houghton Mifflin, 1983.

Scarf, Maggie. "Images That Heal." *Psychology Today* (September 1980): 28–32.

Selye, Hans. *Stress Without Distress.* New York: Lippincott, 1974.

———. *The Stress of Life.* New York: McGraw-Hill, 1978.

Sheinkin, D. *Food, Mind, and Mood.* New York: Warner, 1980.

Shles, L. *Do I Have to Go to School Today?* Rolling Hills Estates, Calif.: Jalmar Press, 1989.

Silberstein, William. *Helping Your Child Grow Slim.* New York: Simon & Schuster, 1982.

Smith, Manuel J. *When I Say No I Feel Guilty.* New York: Bantam, 1975.

Stephens, Ron. "National School Safety Center." *USA Today* (September 23, 1991): 11A.

Stroebel, Charles F. *QR: The Quieting Reflex.* New York: Berkeley, 1982.

Toffler, Alvin. *Future Shock.* New York: Bantam, 1970.

Wallerstein, Judith. *Second Chances: Men, Women, and Children a Decade after Divorce.* in "Learning to Live with a Past That Failed." Boston: Houghton Mifflin, 1990.

Wallis, Claudia. "Stress! Seeking Cures for Modern Anxieties." *Time* (June 6, 1983): 48–54.

Warren, Neil Clark. *Make Anger Your Ally.* Garden City, New York: Doubleday, 1983.

Wassmer, Arthur C. *Making Contact.* New York: Dial, 1978.

Wesley, Frand, and Edith Sullivan. *Human Growth and Development.* 2d ed. New York: Human Science Press, 1986.

Youngs, Bettie B. *Developing Self-Esteem in Your Students.* Rolling Hills Estates, Calif.: Jalmar Press, 1992.

———. *Friendship Is Forever, Isn't It?* Rolling Hills Estates, Calif.: Jalmar Press, 1992.

———. *Goal Setting Skills for Young People.* Rolling Hills Estates, Calif.: Jalmar Press, 1992.

———. *How to Develop Self-Esteem in Your Child: 6 Vital Ingredients.* New York: Fawcett/Columbine, 1991.

———. "The Impact of Stress: Are You Part of a $75 Billion a Year Problem?" *American School and University* (July 1985): 19–23.

———. *Is Your 'Net' Working? A Complete Guide to Building Contacts and Career Visibility.* New York: John Wiley & Sons, 1989.

———. *Keeping Our Children Safe.* Louisville, Kent.: Westminster John Knox Press, 1992.

———. *Problem Solving Skills for Children.* Rolling Hills Estates, Calif.: Jalmar Press, 1992.

———. *Safeguarding Your Teenager from the Dragons of Life: A Guide to the Adolescent Years.* Deerfield Beach, Florida: Health Communications, 1993.

———. *Self-Esteem for Educators: It's Job Criteria #1.* Rolling Hills Estates, Calif.: Jalmar Press, 1992.

———. *Stress Management for Educators: A Guide to Managing Your Response to Stress.* Rolling Hills Estates, Calif.: Jalmar Press, 1992.

———. *A Stress Management Guide for Young People.* Rolling Hills Estates, Calif.: Jalmar Press, 1992.

———. "Utilizing Stress: A Positive Source of Vitality for Educators." *Delta Kappa Gamma Journal* 49 (Winter 1983): 34–39.

———. *You & Self-Esteem: A Book for Young People (Grades 5–12).* Rolling Hills Estates, Calif.: Jalmar Press, 1992.

Help Organizations

Many organizations, some with toll-free 800 phone numbers, provide helpful information:

Adults Molested as Children United (AMACU) is a self-help program for adults who were sexually abused as children. Members work in weekly therapy groups to resolve the problems and conflicts that the sexual abuse has caused in their lives. To find a local AMACU group, or for referrals to local sexual-abuse treatment specialists, consult your telephone directory.

Alcoholics Anonymous, General Service Board, New York, NY 10016. Alcoholics Anonymous is an international fellowship of men and women who share the common problem of alcoholism. Family members of alcoholics can receive help through groups associated with Alcoholics Anonymous, mainly Al-Anon and Al-Ateen (Al-Ateen, Al-Anon Family Group Headquarters, P.O. Box 182, New York, NY 10159–0182). Local Al-Ateen chapters are listed in some telephone directories, or contact a local Al-Anon group for more information.

Big Brothers/Big Sisters of America. Families and single parents under stress can find extra support and occasional respite from parenting responsibilities through this program. Under the direction of professionally trained staff, volunteers support families by working with children in need of additional attention and friendship. Call the local agency listed in your telephone book.

Child Find, Inc. 7 Innis Avenue, New Paltz, NY 12561, (212) 245-6200 or (914) 255-1848.

Family Service America (FSA), (800) 221-2681. FSA is a membership organization of agencies that deal with family problems. It serves more than a thousand communities throughout the United States and Canada. Member agencies serve families and individuals through counseling, advocacy, and family-life education.

Family Stress: Check the telephone directory or contact the United Way organization in your area for a family services agency near you. These organizations offer a variety of counseling services.

National Anorexic Aid Society (NAAS), 1925 E. Granville Rd., Columbus, OH, (614) 436–1112.

The National Center for Missing and Exploited Children, (800) 843-5678. The center assists families, citizens' groups, law enforcement agencies, and governmental institutions, collecting information that could lead to the location and recovery of a missing child.

National Child Abuse Hotline, (800) 422-4453. The National Child Abuse Hotline handles crisis calls and provides information and referrals for every county in the United States. The hotline, a program of Childhelp USA in Woodland Hills, California, also provides literature about child abuse prevention.

National Clearinghouse for Alcohol Information, (301) 468-2600. NCAI is a service of the National Institute of Alcohol Abuse and Alcoholism. The clearinghouse collects worldwide information on studies and programs pertaining to prevention, training, treatment, and research aspects of alcohol abuse and alcoholism and shares this knowledge with interested professionals and the general public.

National Coalition against Domestic Violence, (202) 293-8860. The coalition is a membership organization composed of independently operated shelters for battered women and their families as well as for individuals. To locate a shelter in your area, contact the coalition in Washington, D.C.

National Drug Abuse Hotline, (800) COCAINE. The National Drug Abuse Hotline is a drug-abuse treatment, referral (including local referral), and information service. It provides confidential help for drug abusers and other concerned individuals.

National Institute on Drug Abuse, P.O. Box 2305, Rockville, MD 20852.

National Runaway Switchboard, (800) 621-4000. A toll-free service offering crisis help and referrals nationwide.

National Youth Work Alliance, 1346 Connecticut Ave., N.W., Washington, D.C. 20036. Write to the alliance for the name of a runaway or teen crisis shelter in your area.

Parents Anonymous (P.A.), (800) 352-0386 (in California), (800) 421-0353 (elsewhere). P.A. is a self-help program for parents under stress and for abused children. There are no fees, and no one is required to reveal his or her name. Group members support and encourage each other in searching out positive alternatives to the abusive behavior in their lives.

Stepfamily Association of America, (301) 823-7570. The national Stepfamily Association provides information about local chapters and issues a newsletter. Local chapters offer classes, workshops, and support groups for blended families. Some classes, workshops, and services are free.

Suicide Prevention: Almost every state has one or more suicide hotlines and suicide prevention centers. Check your local phone directory or ask an operator for the hotline number in your area.

Index

About the Author

BETTIE B. YOUNGS, PH.D., ED.D., is an internationally known lecturer, author, counselor, and consultant. Her work has spanned more than sixty countries for more than two decades, earning her a reputation as a respected authority. She has earned national acclaim for her work on the effects of stress on health, wellness, and productivity for both adults and children, and for her work on the role of self-esteem as it detracts from or empowers vitality, achievement, and peak performance.

Dr. Youngs is a former teacher-of-the-year, professor at San Diego State University, and executive director of the Phoenix Foundation. She is the author of fourteen books published in twenty-three languages, as well as a number of popular audio cassette programs. As a member of the National Speakers Association, Dr. Youngs addresses audiences throughout the United States and abroad, meeting with nearly 250,000 youth and adults each year. She serves on the board of directors for the National Council for Self-Esteem and is a frequent guest on radio and television talk shows.

For more information about Dr. Youngs's books, audio tapes, and lectures, contact:

Bettie B. Youngs & Associates
Instruction & Professional Development, Inc.
Suite 100–104
3060 Racetrack View Drive
Del Mar, CA 92014
(619) 481-6360

Printed in the United States
by Baker & Taylor Publisher Services